Praise for Hacking Marketing

"We've long talked about how marketing success is based on the experience it delivers, and now Scott Brinker lays out a terrific manifesto about how to rethink the operations underlying it. He uses his encyclopedic knowledge of the marketing technology world to nail the parallels between marketing and the emerging practices in software development—agile, fast, open, iterative—and translates them in practical approaches to driving change in one's own company. *Hacking Marketing* lays out the implicit principles that have been guiding much of our own work at McKinsey with clients on piloting new marketing operations techniques—storytelling, scrum masters, product management discipline, and especially relentless A/B testing—and makes the logic for doing so incredibly clear. In many ways, Scott is not just talking about hacking 'marketing,' but also addressing the changes to come across most business functions."
—**David C. Edelman**, global co-leader, McKinsey Digital, Marketing and Sales, McKinsey & Company

"*Hacking Marketing* not only creates a compelling model for how to think about the intersection of marketing and our digital world; it helped me rethink the way I approach my role as a CMO. I've asked my entire team to read it."
—**John L. Kennedy**, CMO, Xerox Corporation

"Marketing is going through a seismic change. The change is driven by consumers who are no longer passive in their relationship with brands, technology, and data. *Hacking Marketing* provides a brilliant road map on how to evolve the capability and culture of marketing practices using parallels from the most disruptive industry in the world, the software industry."
—**Ram Krishnan**, SVP and CMO, PepsiCo

"No business function today is more dynamic than marketing. *Hacking Marketing* is a must-read operating manual for CMOs who want to lead in the digital age."

—**Ajay Agarwal**, managing director, Bain Capital Ventures

"We are all digital now. Scott makes it easier than ever for smart marketers to ask the right questions and to discover what they need to know now."

—**Seth Godin**, author, *All Marketers Are Liars*

"An original take on how the management of marketing must transform to keep pace with our increasingly digital world. It's a must-read for anyone looking to stay relevant in this modern marketing era."

—**Ann Handley**, chief content officer, MarketingProfs

"An inspiring read for anyone who wants to master the art and science of modern marketing management, from the practice of lean and agile marketing to the design of a scalable engine for marketing innovation."

—**Mayur Gupta**, SVP and head of Digital, Healthgrades

"The CMOs of tomorrow will be very different from the ones of yesterday. Scott shows how great marketing management today is closer to modern software development than the marketing of yesterday and helps marketers understand how to incorporate those principles to succeed."

—**Rishi Dave**, CMO, Dun & Bradstreet

"The truth is that marketing has changed, more than almost any other profession, and the majority of marketers have no idea how to effectively manage the process. *Hacking Marketing* gives you a flashlight and shows you the truth so you never have to look back again."

—**Joe Pulizzi**, founder, Content Marketing Institute

"I am a strong believer that Agile has to be the foundation of any successful marketing team. Agile will allow marketing executives to have more visibility, increased productivity, and higher profitability. Scott's book provides timely insight into how to make a shift to agile marketing."

—**Joe Staples**, CMO, Workfront

SCOTT BRINKER

HACKING
MARKETING

AGILE PRACTICES TO
MAKE MARKETING
SMARTER, FASTER,
AND MORE INNOVATIVE

WILEY

Cover design: Paul McCarthy

Copyright © 2016 by Scott Brinker. All rights reserved.

Published by John Wiley & Sons, Inc., Hoboken, New Jersey.
Published simultaneously in Canada.

No part of this publication may be reproduced, stored in a retrieval system, or transmitted in any form or by any means, electronic, mechanical, photocopying, recording, scanning, or otherwise, except as permitted under Section 107 or 108 of the 1976 United States Copyright Act, without either the prior written permission of the Publisher, or authorization through payment of the appropriate per-copy fee to the Copyright Clearance Center, 222 Rosewood Drive, Danvers, MA 01923, (978) 750-8400, fax (978) 646-8600, or on the Web at www.copyright.com. Requests to the Publisher for permission should be addressed to the Permissions Department, John Wiley & Sons, Inc., 111 River Street, Hoboken, NJ 07030, (201) 748-6011, fax (201) 748-6008, or online at www.wiley.com/go/permissions.

Limit of Liability/Disclaimer of Warranty: While the publisher and author have used their best efforts in preparing this book, they make no representations or warranties with respect to the accuracy or completeness of the contents of this book and specifically disclaim any implied warranties of merchantability or fitness for a particular purpose. No warranty may be created or extended by sales representatives or written sales materials. The advice and strategies contained herein may not be suitable for your situation. You should consult with a professional where appropriate. Neither the publisher nor the author shall be liable for damages arising herefrom.

For general information about our other products and services, please contact our Customer Care Department within the United States at (800) 762-2974, outside the United States at (317) 572-3993 or fax (317) 572-4002.

Wiley publishes in a variety of print and electronic formats and by print-on-demand. Some material included with standard print versions of this book may not be included in e-books or in print-on-demand. If this book refers to media such as a CD or DVD that is not included in the version you purchased, you may download this material at http://booksupport.wiley.com. For more information about Wiley products, visit www.wiley.com.

Library of Congress Cataloging-in-Publication Data:

Names: Brinker, Scott, 1971- author.
Title: Hacking marketing : agile practices to make marketing smarter, faster, and more innovative / Scott Brinker.
Description: Hoboken, New Jersey : John Wiley & Sons, Inc., [2016] | Includes bibliographical references and index.
Identifiers: LCCN 2015046840 (print) | LCCN 2016002280 (ebook) | ISBN 9781119183174 (hardback) | ISBN 9781119183211 (pdf) | ISBN 9781119183235 (epub)
Subjects: LCSH: Marketing. | Marketing–Management. | BISAC: BUSINESS & ECONOMICS / Marketing / General.
Classification: LCC HF5415 .B6675 2016 (print) | LCC HF5415 (ebook) | DDC 658.8–dc23
LC record available at http://lccn.loc.gov/2015046840

Printed in the United States of America.

10 9 8 7 6 5 4 3 2 1

For Jordan:
Let your imagination always lift you beyond the limits of labels.

And for my parents,
who ran a Mad Men–era marketing agency and encouraged me
to study computer science.

Contents

Introduction

It's a fascinating time to work in marketing.

It's also a somewhat dizzying time, with so much change happening around us.

The world is becoming more digital every day, steadily reshaping relationships between customers and businesses in the process. Buyers have more information, more options, and more leverage in when, where, and how they engage with sellers. And their expectations are rising, as state-of-the-art, digitally native companies—from Amazon.com to Uber—push the limits of what is possible into what is desired and then demanded.

For some businesses, that may still seem like a far-off, foreign realm. Not many of us aim to compete with those digital wunderkinder. Yet every day, we see more signs of digital dynamics infiltrating the space between us and our customers, disrupting sales and marketing in a thousand small ways—and not-so-small ways. We feel the tremors of our competitive landscape shifting.

On closer inspection, that realm is not so far-off after all.

The fact is that in a digital world, inherently, *we are all entangled in digital dynamics.*

"How did my business go digital?" With apologies to Ernest Hemingway, "Two ways. Gradually, then suddenly." Regardless of size, geography, or industry, the digital age is upon us.

The accelerating tempo and growing complexity that this brings—especially to marketing—is both exhilarating and exasperating. It is a whirlwind of obstacles and opportunities.

Marketing Management for a Digital World

My goal is to help you harness that digital whirlwind.

Many wonderful books have been published about the many new strategies and tactics of digital marketing—inbound marketing, content marketing, social media marketing, and so on.

But there's a common thread connecting all of them that has received far less attention, yet is crucial to their success: How should *marketing management* evolve to best leverage these modern marketing methods?

Management is the orchestration of *all* those different strategies and tactics. It's how we weave them together into a cohesive organization with a mission and the methods to achieve it.

The trouble is that traditional approaches to marketing management—classic marketing plans, designed and enforced in a siloed, top-down structure—are buckling under the pressures of the digital world. There are too many moving parts, spinning too quickly. Strange interaction effects abound. It can feel like you're driving at high speed with a broken steering wheel and failed brakes. At night. With no headlights.

But there is a bright, shining way forward.

Marketing is not the first profession to struggle with digital dynamics. Before any other discipline found itself roiled by digital turbulence, software development teams ran into many of these issues first. Continuously changing requirements. Rapidly evolving technology. Mounting complexity. And demanding stakeholders who had little appreciation for those difficulties.

Software developers have been the canaries in this coal mine. Through trial and error in millions of software projects, successes and failures, they have discerned some of the underlying patterns of what works and what doesn't—and why—when wrangling the digital dragon. As a result, the art and science of managing software has matured tremendously.

So what does this have to do with marketing?

More than you might think.

The challenges of creating great software and the challenges of creating great marketing share increasing similarities in a digital world. They're both juggling an explosion of digitally powered interactions in a tornado of constant change and innovation. They're both creative and intellectual disciplines that rely on human insight and inspiration, and a new kind of teamwork, to produce remarkable experiences in highly competitive environments. And as the world has grown more digital, the scale and scope of their responsibilities and influence have grown too—but at the cost of mushrooming complexity.

Given those parallels—and the head start that software leaders have had wrestling with these challenges—are there successful, digitally native management concepts from the software community that modern marketers could borrow and adapt to conquer their own digital dragons?

I believe the answer is yes.

Hacking Marketing

This is not a technical book. It assumes no knowledge, or even interest, in software development. All it requires is an open mind to look at marketing management from a different perspective.

Don't be alarmed by the title, *Hacking Marketing*.

As we'll discuss in the first chapter, hacking has a very different meaning in the software community than it does in the media. It's not about *breaking*. It's about *making*.

The bad kind of hacking breaks into systems.

The good kind makes new inventions—in fast, fluid, and fun ways. It imagines what's possible, figures out clever ways to realize those ideas within the tangle of real-world constraints, and above all, celebrates the courage to try, tinker, and learn.

Cross-pollinating management concepts between the realms of software and marketing is that good kind of hacking but on an organizational level. And in championing that, we'll strive to bring a touch of kinetic hacker spirit to everything marketing does.

This book is organized into five parts:

I. An orientation on digital dynamics and the parallels between marketing and software
II. An in-depth examination of agile and lean management methods applied to marketing
III. An exploration of opportunities and techniques for innovation in modern marketing
IV. A collection of ideas to tame digital complexity and achieve new kinds of scalability in marketing
V. A closing chapter on managing marketing talent in this digital environment

Part II on agile marketing is the most comprehensive, because that is the foundation on which digitally savvy marketing management must be built. We'll thoroughly cover the rationale and key practices of agile management, specifically in the context of marketing.

Parts III, IV, and V cast a wider net, providing a helicopter tour of a variety of other concepts and frameworks from the field of software management that have become surprisingly relevant to the challenges of modern marketing. We'll approach each of them in a pragmatic and nontechnical way through the lens of how they directly benefit marketing today.

Hacking Marketing aims to expand your mental models as a marketer and a manager for leading marketing in a digital world where everything—especially marketing—now flows with the speed and adaptability of software.

Scott Brinker
chiefmartec.com

I

Marketing ≈ Digital ≈ Software

1

Hacking Is a Good Thing

When most people hear the word *hacking*, they think of something bad.

They picture cybercriminals who break into computer systems to steal credit cards or deface people's websites. They recall sensational news stories, such as the hacking of Sony Pictures Entertainment in 2014, which resulted in the studio's private, internal e-mails being published all over the Internet—to the horrified embarrassment of many Hollywood elites. Or even more serious hacking of government systems by foreign spies.

Hackers, the perpetrators of such digital mischief and mayhem, have frequently been the villains in movies themselves. In *Live Free or Die Hard*—the fourth movie in that storied Bruce Willis franchise—hero cop John McClane battles a hacker bent on bringing the United States to financial ruin by wreaking havoc on the stock market, the power grid, the transportation grid, and other key, computer-controlled components of the nation's infrastructure.

At this point, you may be wondering whether you've mistakenly purchased a book that intends to teach you how to electronically steal your competitors' marketing plans or knock out their marketing systems. Is that what is meant by "hacking marketing"?

Rest assured, no.

There's actually another much more positive meaning of the word *hacking*.

In software development circles, hacking is the art of invention. When a programmer creates a particularly cool piece of software, especially in an inspired burst of coding, that is hacking. When an engineer devises a novel solution to a supposedly intractable problem, that is hacking. When a maker—someone who builds do-it-yourself robots, electronics, and other cool gadgets—fabricates a new homemade design, improvised from ordinary components into a functional work of art, that is hacking.

Picture Mark Zuckerberg, up late at night in his Harvard University dorm room, madly cranking away on building the first version of Facebook. He imagined new ways for people to connect with each other through a website, unconstrained by prior conventions—and launched the golden age of social media.

That is hacking.

In fact, Facebook would take hacking to a whole new level in business management.

Facebook and the Hacker Way

Facebook was founded on the principles of hacking—the good kind of hacking. And that approach to getting things done helped propel it into a $200 billion company.

Indeed, when Facebook filed for its initial public offering in 2012, Zuckerberg wrote an open letter to prospective shareholders, in the S-1 registration statement that the company filed with the Securities and Exchange Commission, describing his vision for the firm.[1] It famously included a section, on pages 69–70, under the heading "The Hacker Way" that explained the company's unique culture—and why it was such a powerful source of competitive advantage.

Zuckerberg countered the negative connotations of hacking as typically portrayed in the media. "Hacking just means building something quickly or testing the boundaries of what can be done." In a little more than 800 words, Zuckerberg described the essence of hacking as a creative force and how it was embedded into the culture and management principles of his company.

"The Hacker Way is an approach to building that involves continuous improvement and iteration. Hackers believe that something can always be better, and that nothing is ever complete. They just have to go fix it—often in the face of people who say it's impossible or are content with the status quo."

He repeatedly emphasized the importance of rapid iterations. "Hackers try to build the best services over the long term by quickly releasing and learning from smaller iterations rather than trying to get everything right all at once."

He championed a software-empowered bias for action. "Instead of debating for days whether a new idea is possible or what the best way to build something is, hackers would rather just prototype something and see what works."

He defined the company's hacker-inspired values around being fast, bold, and open.

For Zuckerberg, being open meant instilling a high level of transparency in the way the company was managed internally, stating a firm belief that the more information people have, the better decisions they can make—and the greater impact they can have. "We work hard to make sure everyone at Facebook has access to as much information as possible about every part of the company so they can make the best decisions and have the greatest impact."

Although Zuckerberg wasn't the first person to champion the hacker ethos—hacking emerged at Massachusetts Institute of Technology (MIT) in the 1960s, 20 years before he was born[2]—this letter to investors, traditionally conservative Wall Street types, was remarkable in presenting it as a mainstream business philosophy. It was a brilliant piece of marketing, positioning the company as an exciting innovator in the digital world. But it was also a management manifesto, declaring that Facebook intended to run its whole business—not just product development—with a hacker mentality.

Idealistic? Perhaps.

But you have to acknowledge Facebook's incredible success. It created a new kind of company, a social media juggernaut, that has had far-reaching, global impact. It sprang from a college sophomore's side project into one of the highest-valued public companies in the world, all in less than a decade. Along the way, it fended off intense competition—in a market that disruptive innovation continually roils—from dozens of aggressive start-ups and even the world's other largest Internet company, Google.

Why This Matters to You

However, odds are your business is not a social media platform like Facebook. Hacking probably sounds like something that's meant for companies with tinkering engineers and Silicon Valley code jockeys. How is it relevant to regular businesses? And what does it have to do with marketing?

Those questions inspired this book.

First, Facebook demonstrated that the spirit of hacking could be adapted and applied to general business management, not just technical innovation. It's not just for techies.

Second, Facebook proved that such a management philosophy was scalable, even for a public company with thousands of employees worldwide. It's not just for start-ups.

And third, even if your company isn't a purely digital business like Facebook, you are now operating in a digital world. Marketing, in particular, has become heavily dependent on digital channels and touchpoints to reach and engage customers—in both consumer and business-to-business markets. As a result, you are affected by digital dynamics, regardless of your industry, size, or location. You have more in common with Facebook than you might think. That might seem like a scary thought at first. But it's really an opportunity.

Digital environments enable far greater agility, innovation, and scalability than were ever possible in just the physical world. But harnessing that potential requires different approaches to management—approaches that leverage digital dynamics instead of fighting them. Luckily, we don't have to figure this out from scratch. We can draw upon more than two decades of management practices that have proved successful in purely digital businesses and professions—particularly in software development—and adapt them for modern marketing management. Modern marketing actually has more similarities with software development management than you might imagine.

This book will show you how to tap those parallels to your advantage.

Hacking marketing is about bringing a little bit of that inventive hacker spirit to the management and practice of marketing. In a digital world, that proves to be a very good thing.

2

Marketing Is a Digital Profession

The central idea of this book—that marketers can benefit by adopting management practices that were forged in the natively digital profession of software development—rests on the premise that marketing has become a digital profession itself.

You may have raised an eyebrow at that assertion. Certainly some elements of marketing are undeniably digital: websites, e-mail, online advertising, search engine marketing, and social media. These are the things that we have labeled as *digital marketing* over the past decade.

But there are still many other facets of marketing that don't appear to be digital in nature. Traditional TV, print, radio, and out-of-home advertising. Trade show events. In-store marketing. Public relations. Brand management. Channel management. Market research. Pricing. How can marketing be considered a digital profession when so many important components of it still operate outside the digital realm?

Marketing in a Digital World

When Clive Sirkin was named the chief marketing officer (CMO) of Kimberly-Clark—the company behind major brands such as Kleenex tissues, Huggies diapers, and Scott paper products—he remarked that it no longer believed in digital marketing but rather marketing in a digital world.[1]

It was a simple yet profound observation.

In most organizations, digital marketing grew up in a silo, separate from the rest of the marketing department. There were usually two reasons for this. First, most businesses didn't rely on digital touchpoints as the primary interface to their prospects and customers. Sure, they had a website, an e-mail subscription list, and maybe some online advertising, but those things weren't seen as the heart of the business. And second, digital marketing required a different set of skills, attracted different kinds of talent to its ranks, and often developed a different subculture from the rest of the marketing team. It was rarely well integrated with other marketing programs, usually had a small budget, and typically wielded little influence on marketing leadership.

But then the world changed.

Smartphones and tablets proliferated, all offering instant, high-speed connectivity to the Internet, wherever you were, whatever you were doing. Search engines, such as Google, became everyone's reflexive go-to source for answers to almost any question. Social media—Facebook, LinkedIn, YouTube, Twitter, Yelp, TripAdvisor, Angie's List, Glassdoor, and hundreds of other specialized sites—triggered a worldwide explosion of information sharing. All kinds of apps, the tiny applications that we download on to our mobile devices, became an ambient part of our lives, at home, work, and school. We became continuously connected to the cloud.

Somewhere around 2012, we reached a tipping point. Digital channels and touchpoints were influencing people's buying decisions for all kinds of products and services, at every stage of the customer life cycle. Such digital interactions were no longer distinct moments either ("I'll go to my computer to check that out online"). They were interwoven into daily life, with the real world and digital world spilling into each other, like hot and cold water mixing in a bath.

Digital dynamics increasingly affected the real world.

This was the brilliant insight in Sirkin's statement. Once buyers stopped treating digital as an isolated channel, but rather as a universal source for information, on-demand service, and social validation for almost *any* purchase decision, brands that continued to relegate digital marketing to something separate from their core marketing mission would do so at their peril.

We're now marketers in a digital world.

Why Marketing Is Now a Digital Profession

Against the backdrop of a digital world, marketing has become a digital profession—and not just in the activities previously classified as digital marketing. There are many ways in which digital dynamics now pervade almost every corner of marketing.

First, the activities that we've explicitly thought of as digital marketing continue to grow as a percentage of marketing investment. The global media firm Carat has estimated that digital advertising spending is growing at double-digit rates, fueled mostly by growth in mobile and online video ads.[2] Forrester Research expects that digital marketing spend will soon exceed TV advertising in the United States.[3] According to an Econsultancy study, 77 percent of marketers increased their digital budgets last year.[4] So obviously, the more purely digital marketing work we do, the more marketing is inherently a digital profession.

Second, marketing touchpoints in the real world are increasingly connected to the digital world. Quick response (QR) codes, one of the first inventions to bridge the digital and the physical, link printed materials to websites. Bluetooth beacons, installed in stores and at live events, automatically trigger offers and other location-based services for people on their mobile devices. Electronic tags attached to tangible goods and physical installations—using radio-frequency identification (RFID) or near field communication (NFC) technology—make them digitally visible for channel management, point-of-sale promotions, and postsale relationships with customers. Mobile apps produced by airlines, hotels, and retailers act on a consumer's global positioning system (GPS) location to enable special features and benefits. Wi-Fi–enabled appliances and gadgets are even creating new marketing touchpoints embedded in people's lives. A good example is the Amazon Dash Button, a physical button that consumers can press to instantly reorder common household goods, such as a Tide laundry detergent button affixed to their washing machine. So formerly nondigital marketing channels are acquiring digital dimensions for us to manage.

Third, digital business transformation—taking a nondigital business and remaking its offerings and operations to take advantage of digital technologies—now affects nearly every industry. Some of the most fascinating examples of this are digital layers juxtaposed on top of the physical world that have disrupted major markets. For instance, Uber rocked the taxi industry by using mobile apps, location data, and digital payments and profiles to orchestrate drivers and riders in a new kind of transportation network. (Taxis are now fighting back by deploying apps of their own.) But there are plenty of more mundane examples where consumers simply expect to be able to learn detailed information about a business and its offerings, conduct transactions, and resolve customer service issues on the Web or through a mobile app. These digital business features go beyond marketing, of course. But it is—or should be—marketing's responsibility to understand, champion, and promote this new wave of digitally enabled customer experiences.

Fourth, thanks to search engines and social media, even businesses with nothing digital about their actual products or services are affected by the way their companies are represented on the Internet. It's not just about what you officially publish online. It's mostly about what *other* people—customers, partners, employees, and influencers of all kinds—say about you on their blogs, in online reviews, and across social networks. Opinions of your business, good or bad, can be shared instantly, spread virally, and last forever in a Google search result. Everything you do in marketing today is subject to these digital feedback effects. You can spend months producing a high-end TV advertising campaign, but within minutes, your audience can commend or crucify you for it on social media, with far greater impact than the airtime you purchased. Marketing must be tuned into these digital conversations and be able to engage effectively with them.

And fifth, as Figure 2.1 shows, marketing now relies on a tremendous amount of digital infrastructure behind the scenes to manage its operations. As marketers, we're inundated with software applications in our daily work. Our toolbox has come a long way from containing simply Excel and Photoshop. Today, we use specialized software for analytics, campaign management, content management, digital asset management, programmatic advertising, customer relationship management, marketing resource management, and more. We are a digital profession in no small part because we spend so much of our day working with these digital tools. We're affected by the digital dynamics of those tools themselves—such as the rapid update cycles that software-as-a-service products typically have. But more important, these tools have the potential to give us digital leverage—speed, scale, adaptability, adjacency, and precision—in so many of our back-office processes.

I say "potential" in that last sentence, because to achieve that digital leverage, we often have to rethink the way we work to really take advantage of these new capabilities. We have to adopt digital management practices.

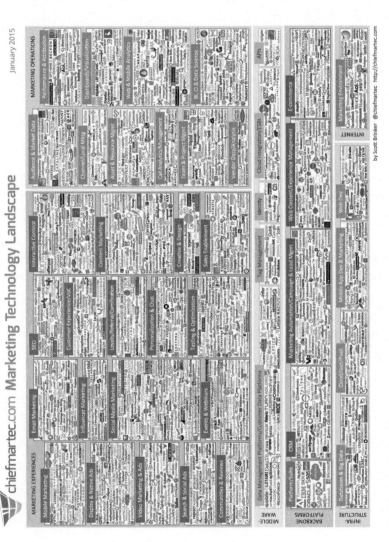

FIGURE 2.1 Marketing Technology Landscape

Note: *SEO* stands for search engine optimization, *VoC* stands for voice of the customer, *BI* for business intelligence, *CI* for commercial intelligence, *ESB* for enterprise service bus, *API* for application programming interface, *CRM* for customer relationship management, *IaaS* for infrastructure as a service, and *PaaS* for platform as a service.

3

What Exactly Are *Digital Dynamics?*

W e've seen that marketing is now a digital profession, and we touched on some of the ways it is affected by digital dynamics. But what exactly are *digital dynamics*?

Five characteristics of the digital world cause it to behave quite differently than the physical world: speed, adaptability, adjacency, scale, and precision. Digital dynamics are the effects these properties generate, and much of the power of digital comes from these features and what they make possible.

But it's difficult to harness that power through management practices that were designed in a predigital world. It's like trying to fly a plane by reading the driver's manual for a car. Yes, they're both transportation, but you're dealing with a different set of levers and gauges—and some very different physics. Running a digital profession by the rules of nondigital management imposes artificial limits on what we can do and leads to organizational dissonance.

Instead, we want management methods that can leverage digital dynamics, rather than struggle against them.

So let us briefly examine each of these five digital characteristics, graphically represented in Figure 3.1, to make sure that we

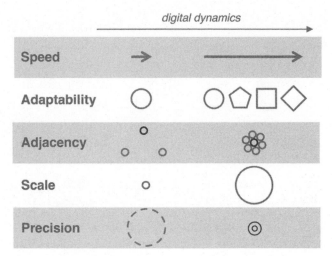

FIGURE 3.1   Five Digital Dynamics: Speed, Adaptability, Adjacency, Scale, and Precision

recognize them and appreciate their effects. This will then help us evaluate existing management approaches—as well as new ones, designed for this new environment—with digital dynamics in mind.

Speed

If there's one overarching factor that dominates digital, it's speed.

Communication happens faster now than ever in human history. We can instantly fire up Internet videoconferences with people halfway around the world, at any time—essentially for free. In social media, everything from breaking news to silly memes can spread to millions of people in a matter of minutes. Even in the more modest context of most businesses, word can swiftly spread across relevant audiences—in reviews, comments, and popular posts—for better or worse. As marketers, we have the option to immediately e-mail an announcement to our entire universe, at least to anyone whose e-mail address we have. That's incredible power, but one that is also easily abused (*"Please* stop spamming me!").

We can access information faster than ever before too. Google has set the expectation that we can find almost anything on the Web, any time we want it. Closely related is increasing computational speed—as computers continue to get more powerful, they can calculate answers to harder problems and process larger and more complicated tasks for us, faster.

These phenomena have combined to feed a *culture of now.* We expect to be able to go to an insurance company's website and get a quote on demand, as fast as we can fill in a form. And the shorter the form is, the better, because we want to move faster. It's quite a contrast with scheduling an appointment to sit down with an insurance agent in a week.

Perhaps the scariest thing in a digital world is the speed at which things change. Markets, opinions, competition, expectations, opportunities—all evolve at an incredibly rapid pace. This is partly because of the speed of communications and information access and partly because of the exponential rate at which technology is advancing. We'll dig deeper into that later in this book, because it greatly affects how we should think about managing innovation.

To be sure, this acceleration of business and life that digital speed enables isn't always a good thing. Our challenge in digital management is often twofold: (1) How do we execute faster, when an increased tempo benefits us, yet (2) how do we resist unwise knee-jerk reactions or overheated churn in our strategy?

Adaptability

An almost-magical quality of the digital world is how malleable, or adaptable, it is.

For instance, you can change the content on your website at any time, right away, with incredible ease. You probably take that for granted—updating a website seems pretty mundane at this point—but there's nothing in the physical world that can be altered that effortlessly. How long would it take you to reorganize a storefront, reprint brochures, swap out a new (nondigital) billboard advertisement, or construct a new trade show booth?

In practice though, how easily you can manipulate your website depends on the software you are using, the rules and processes your company requires you to follow to do so, and your relevant knowledge and skills. The time and expense for making website changes are almost all a function of human and organizational factors—while the costs of distributing them on the Web are, technically speaking, close to zero. This will be a recurring theme: how can we reduce unnecessary organizational constraints to take maximum advantage of digital malleability.

But digital is even more adaptable than that, because changes don't have to be manually designed and deployed, one at a time, by humans at all. Software can automatically change our website for us. Personalization algorithms automatically swap in different content for different visitors, depending on their expressed or predicted preferences. A/B testing software alternates different versions of content to visitors to determine which is most effective at influencing their behavior. Responsive design adjusts how content appears to visitors on different devices, from small smartphone screens to big desktop monitors. There can be hundreds, thousands, or even millions of variations of your website without you having to explicitly define each one.

This is amazing, but it can also be challenging to wrap our heads around and to learn how to manage. We're used to a world where there is one objective reality. If you and I both walk into the same store, at the same time, we will see the same promotional display. But in the digital world, adaptability means that everyone in our audience—and even people on our own staff—may be presented with very different experiences.

The examples above are for websites, but this same adaptability applies to anything that is digital or digitally supported:

mobile apps, online advertising, or even call scripts that dynamically appear on a customer service representative's computer.

Adjacency

The concept of distance in the digital world, for everything connected to the Internet, is rather strange. You can jump from one website to another just by clicking a link or typing a new Web address into your browser. The businesses behind those sites may be on opposite sides of the world, but that doesn't matter. Digital distance is simply the number of electronic steps you have to take—clicks, searches, requests for recommendations from your social networks, and so on—before you find what you want.

This has thoroughly disrupted the nature of competition. Prospects can hop over to a competitor's website in an instant. They can engage in *showrooming*—browsing products in a physical store, then ordering from a cheaper provider, often right there on their mobile phone. Competitors can buy advertising that shows up when people search for keywords related to someone else's business. They can insert themselves into discussions about rivals happening on social media. Any scrappy start-up can use these tactics against competitors many times their size. Digital adjacency has enabled a whole new generation of guerrilla marketing.

It's also demolished the information asymmetry that sellers used to have over buyers. In earlier days, buyers had to rely heavily on a business's salespeople to answer questions they had, especially for complicated purchases, such as in business-to-business buying decisions. Today, buyers answer most of their questions themselves on the Internet, where they can look up details about solutions, compare alternatives, find out what other customers have to say, and research a near-limitless amount of information around a buying decision. Buyers still consume marketing-produced content and engage with salespeople—but they don't rely on them to the same degree that they used to. The adjacency of a digital world puts immense market knowledge at their fingertips.

Digital adjacency can also be harnessed inside an organization. We can connect internal teams to more information, services, and collaborators than ever before. Intranets, wikis, enterprise social networks, dashboards, and other shared applications and databases can help employees break out of silos and better leverage the collective knowledge of the whole firm. The technical work to do this is relatively easy. The challenges are changing processes, policies, and patterns of behavior to permit and encourage this—developing a corporate culture that fosters greater openness and collaboration.

Adjacency engenders transparency, a transformative force in markets and organizations. But management techniques that were forged in a predigital age of less transparency must be rethought and relinquished. As we'll see, this actually becomes a central factor in improving marketing agility.

Scale

The digital world scales very differently, too.

Content on your website can be consumed by 10 people or 10 million with not much of a difference in expense. You may need additional bandwidth and servers, but relative to physical media—say, printing and delivering more catalogs—marginal digital costs are small. The hard part is coming up with content that 10 million people would *want* to consume.

More broadly, information about your company—not just what you publish but also what others share—can be widely distributed through search engines and social media. Thanks to the properties of speed and adjacency, content or information that is especially interesting can go viral and quickly spread to a massive number of people. The Internet as a whole robustly handles such rapid shifts in interest at scale by diffusing copies and related conversations across a myriad of websites. (Individual websites and services are considered *Web scale* if they're able to directly withstand such peaks in demand on their own.)

The downside to this distributed scalability of information is that it defies centralized control. Once something spreads, it's impossible to erase it from the Web's collective memory simply by pressing a delete button.

Digital storage also grows at a scale that has no parallel in the physical world. We're able to store ever-larger quantities of digital assets and data for progressively shrinking costs. Every year, we generate more content, collect more data, and retain it all longer. The life span of digital objects is asymptotically approaching forever. This is the engine of *big data*—and the curse of information overload.

Computational power is another kind of digital scalability. As computer algorithms replace humans for more and more tasks, they usually do those tasks much faster and cheaper— often by many orders of magnitude. For instance, when manual lead scoring is replaced by automated predictive analytics, lead processing can grow, accelerate, and factor in more variables. Software can crunch data on a scale far beyond our own mental abilities. Indeed, one of the societal challenges of the twenty-first century is dealing with the consequences of machines being able to do more of the jobs that used to be doable only by people.

There are limits to digital scale, of course. But the bottlenecks are typically where the real world and the digital world intersect. As humans, we can consume only so much information and content in one day. We can also impose limits on a digital process by inserting steps that require a person to contribute input or approve an action. In some cases, such human intervention is wise—in others, it unnecessarily slows things down. Finding the right balance between automated scale and human judgment is an evolving management challenge.

Precision

Finally, digital is incredibly precise when it comes to quantifying objects and actions.

It's very easy to count things that happen in a digital environment—clicks, impressions, visits, minutes spent on a website, downloads, app installs, transactions, and so on. Thanks to the characteristic of scale just discussed, we can automatically record almost everything and perform all kinds of calculations on that data. Those computations are highly reliable.[1]

Such precision is why digital marketing is celebrated as being so measurable. We can track what prospects and customers do across the different digital touchpoints they have with us and use this information to determine what seems to be working—or not working—in our marketing programs. We can run experiments and A/B tests to improve those touchpoints quantifiably. And we can use such details collected about individuals, and others seemingly similar to them, to personalize how we engage with them, thanks to digital's adaptability.

Of course, this is bigger than just digital marketing. We now have access to a tremendous amount of data across all aspects of our businesses, which we can use to inform the decisions we make. Data-driven management has grown as a powerful movement to embrace more analytical methods in leadership, countering our mental biases and gut-feel guesses.

There are great benefits to being more data driven but also cautions to heed. Just because we have a *lot* of data doesn't mean that we have *all* the data relevant to a particular decision. One of the reasons that calculating true attribution and return on investment in marketing is still a hard problem is because we don't have data on the things that influence prospects besides the touchpoints we (or those willing to share data) are able to observe. Crucially, we don't have data from inside people's heads—well, at least not yet—to know the weights they assign to those different influences and how they all combine into a final decision.

We still need to apply judgment in many data-driven management decisions—including the choice of which data to use and how to interpret it. Because there's so much data out there, it is easy to go hunting for data to bolster almost any argument. (Being data driven shouldn't mean driving around until you find data that supports your opinion.) It's worth considering the biases inherent in how a particular set of data was collected and other factors that affect data quality. Most of all, the responsibility remains on us to *ask the right questions*—or we can end up with answers that have a high degree of precision while steering us woefully in the wrong direction.

As with the other digital characteristics, the staggering abundance of precisely quantified data affects how we can—and should—manage marketing in a digital world.

These are digital dynamics. And they are wild and wondrous.

4

Marketing Is Now Deeply Entwined with Software

Everything digital is controlled by software.

That might seem obvious. But software defines and operates literally *everything* in the digital world. Software is more than just the applications we install on our computers and smartphones. Every website and online service we use, from Amazon.com to Yahoo!, is a software program—or, more accurately, usually a whole collection of software programs working together. Every digital device in our lives runs software that determines how it behaves—including many things that you wouldn't normally think of, such as cars. Chevrolet's early electric car, the Volt, was reported to have more than 10 million lines of code built into its systems.[1]

People talk a lot about the explosion of data in the digital world. Admittedly, there is a staggering amount of data out there—a figure now measured in yottabytes, a unit equal to 1 quadrillion (that's 1,000 trillion) gigabytes each. But data by itself is inert. It just sits where it is stored. It's *software* that generates all of that data and processes it to do something useful.

It is the explosion of software that's truly astounding. It has been estimated that possibly over a trillion of lines of code have been written by software developers.[2] And if you count all the copies of that code, as software programs are installed on billions of different devices, you realize that our world is indeed consumed by software.

We say we live in a digital world. But equivalently, we live in a *software world*.

Software Is Modern Marketing's Middleman

Digital marketing has generally been thought of as a form of direct marketing. We think of it as *direct* because interactions between marketers and audiences can happen with no apparent intermediaries in seconds—or even fractions of a second. We control what we send down the wire. No one acts as a middleman between us.

Or so it might seem from a distance.

In truth, as shown in Figure 4.1, digital marketing has dynamics that are more like channel marketing than you might recognize at first. The digital pathway from marketers to their audience is not a physical channel of humans, such as distributors and retailers. Instead, it's a digital channel of software. Even though marketing travels through that channel instantaneously, it still passes through multiple independent layers—a whole series of software programs—each of which can influence the interaction. We don't have as much control over the digital channel as we'd like to believe.

To start, there's all the software that we use to create and manage our digital marketing campaigns: creative design tools, website content management systems, marketing automation platforms, programmatic advertising solutions, customer relationship management databases, and so on. As we noted in Chapter 2, we are inundated with software for almost all the tasks we do in marketing today.

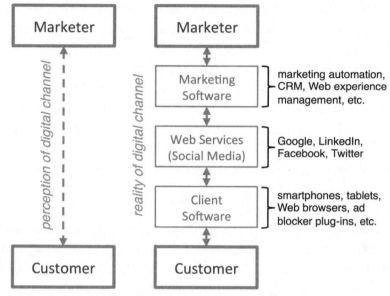

FIGURE 4.1 Digital Marketing Is a Software-Mediated Channel
Note: *CRM* stands for customer relationship management.

It's important to realize that the software we choose to use—or are required to use by choices other people in our organization have made—has a material impact on our marketing.

In a digital world, software is our eyes and ears for observing what people in our audience are doing. For instance, consider something as simple as Web analytics. The way your particular Web analytics software chooses to track and aggregate data, how it lets you visualize that data, the options it gives you for customizing reports—all of these things will affect your perceptions of what you see in activity on your website. In turn, that will influence the decisions you make based on that information. Software is also our *hands* by which we touch our audience through a digital channel. Here too, the particular software you purchase—depending on its capabilities, its user interface, and what it makes easy or hard to do—will shape what you deliver through this channel.

Even when we exert control over which software we adopt and what we consciously do with it, we still aren't fully in control of this layer of our digital channel. The technology vendors who design that software—and usually continue to update it—implicitly affect our marketing by the choices they make too. And not all of their choices are readily apparent to us, because they may be technical details embedded deep inside their implementations. It's important to recognize that we can encounter unexpected behaviors or effects at this layer of our digital channel at any time, and we should be prepared to detect and react to them.

The next layer of software in our digital channel is made up of the independent Internet services, mostly social media, that frequently serve as a conduit for interactions between us and our audience—Google, Facebook, LinkedIn, Twitter, and so on. Although we can sometimes bypass this layer if a customer is engaged with us directly through our owned media, such as our website, we often rely on interactions with customers through these independent earned and paid media sites and services to bring people to our website. We either have to *earn* the right to be present in these services—through some combination of how worthy each service or its users deem us to be—or *pay* for that privilege.

For example, with Google, we can earn a top ranking in the organic search results for a particular keyword by producing popular content, or we can bid for a paid ad to accompany those results. They're both ways to drive people to our own website. But if we're not present on that results page in some fashion, then people searching for products or services associated with that keyword may never find us. As a rough analogy to the distribution of consumer packaged goods, we need to be stocked on those digital shelves, so to speak, at the locations that people look for such things. This layer of the digital channel wields enormous power.

All of these Internet services are software programs—often, technically, a collection of many interrelated software programs, orchestrated around a common mission. This means that they exude the strange digital dynamics of speed, scale, adjacency, and so on that we discussed in the previous chapter. In particular, they can change very quickly. Facebook has stated that it updates new releases of its software twice a day.[3] Amazon.com reportedly pushes new software code live every 11.6 seconds.[4]

Because these software programs dictate the rules by which you and your audience interact through them, any of those updates can have an impact on your business. If Google changes its search algorithms, and suddenly your site drops in its rankings, that can be devastating to your business. A change that Google made last year to promote mobile-friendly websites was known as *Mobilegeddon*—an Armageddon reference—for its punishing consequences on websites that didn't embrace mobile Web support quickly enough. Many scrambled to do just that. But most of the changes that ripple across these Internet services are not announced with that level of fanfare. As with the previous layer, our internally adopted marketing software, we must be vigilant to detect and react to shifting behaviors in this Web services layer of our channel.

The final layer of the digital channel, the critical last mile, consists of all the software that our prospects and customers run. This includes their choice of Web browser, their choice of smartphone, the apps they install, and any ad blocking or e-mail spam detection filters that they enable. Most of them probably don't explicitly think of these things as software. They have simply become ambient features of modern life that most people take for granted.

But these are software programs. Depending on how they're programmed and configured, they shape and filter the way in which your audience interacts with you digitally. As marketers, we are subjugated by their rules. And like all the other layers of this digital channel, this software can change swiftly and suddenly too—forcing us to adapt or risk losing connections with our customers.

When you step back to admire this entire of chain of software that controls every layer of the digital marketing channel, it's rather breathtaking. And scary. Because it becomes clear just how dependent on software marketing has become for the digital relationships with our audience.

Marketing Is a Software-Powered Discipline

Just as marketing should understand any other channel that it depends upon to reach and engage customers, it should understand this software-driven, digital pipeline too.

That doesn't mean that everyone in marketing needs to become a software engineer. (Although marketing technologists—marketers with software expertise—are increasingly an important part of marketing teams.) However, it does mean that marketing must understand how to harness this software-powered channel effectively. What's possible? What fits our strategy? Or, in some cases, how should we shift our strategy to fit this environment? How do we implement our strategy in this software-based setting?

Most of all, how should we adjust *marketing management* in a world dominated by digital dynamics to take full advantage of its power and potential?

We're almost ready to answer that question. But there's one more piece of the puzzle that we must acknowledge. Marketing today does more than just use software and rely on it as a channel for reaching customers. It now builds software too.

5

Marketers Are Software Creators Now

You might not realize it at first, but modern marketing teams don't just *use* software these days—they create it too. Quite a bit of it, actually.

What is software, anyway? A software program is simply a set of instructions that tells computers, or other digital devices, what to do. You can manually launch these programs, such as when you tap an icon on your smartphone to open up your e-mail app. Some software programs can also be configured to run automatically at regular intervals or when some external event happens—such as when a prospect visits your website.

Software programs can also interact with other software programs. The term *API*, which stands for application programming interface—a term that marketers hear more frequently these days—describes the ways a software program makes itself available for such interactions. If a software program can be mostly controlled through its APIs, it's considered *open*. If not, it is considered a *closed* system. As you might imagine, with all the different software programs in the digital marketing channel that we examined in the previous chapter, open APIs have become increasingly important to orchestrating all these different pieces.

The big picture here is that most software operates in layers. If you want to visualize a large layer cake, that's not a bad metaphor. Layers above use the layers below as services that help them accomplish a higher-level mission. Just as the very top of a cake has a layer of icing—which is the best part, of course—in software, the top layer is the highest level of instructions being given to the system.

I know, that sounds kind of techy. But here's the twist: In today's digital environment, *marketers* are often the people programming that top layer. They just don't always know it.

Marketing-Managed Software Projects

First, we should acknowledge that marketing now often leads a number of projects that are explicitly recognized as software development.

Websites are the most common example. For many years, marketers mostly concerned themselves with only the *design* of their company's website—the way individual pages looked—and the *content* inserted into pages, primarily static text, photographs, and illustrations. But websites today are often much more sophisticated. They include *functionality* to let customers place orders, make customer service requests, and check on the status of their accounts. Prospects can engage with interactive content, such as assessment tools, calculators, and configurators. A modern website often doesn't consist of just individual pages but also multistep flows that visitors must go through to accomplish tasks, such as signing up for a service.

These kinds of websites are effectively built as software development projects. Typically, they use a combination of off-the-shelf software enhanced with custom programming to provide the functionality that is specific to that business. Many software-related disciplines are usually brought together: programmers, user experience (UX) designers, database administrators, and systems administrators. On smaller projects, one developer may wear several of those hats.

For many marketers, building such a website is often their first exposure to working with software developers. If you've been through one of these projects, you may have been introduced to *agile* software development methods. You may have seen preliminary *prototypes* of your website. You may have launched your website in a *beta* mode while problems, or *bugs*, were identified and fixed. These are terms and concepts from the software profession that have made their way into our everyday language. Because we now live in a digital world, where software is everywhere, we find ourselves using these words in regular conversations.

Beyond websites, we increasingly engage in other software development projects, such as mobile apps for smartphones and tablets. We may oversee the development of software for in-store kiosks. We may have custom software built for use behind-the-scenes to manage databases or to generate specialized reports. Of course, in most instances, we as marketers are not actually writing the code for this software. Instead, we work closely with software engineers who create these programs to our specifications.

However, there are many cases today of marketers personally programming software that we don't necessarily recognize as software development—but pragmatically speaking, it is.

Marketing Automation Is Programming

Marketing automation software has become popular in recent years. Features vary widely from one solution to the next, but generally such software lets marketers automate campaigns to respond to prospect behaviors. For instance, if prospects visit your website and provide their e-mail address in exchange for downloading an e-book, then your marketing automation software can automatically queue them up to receive follow-up e-mail messages. Depending on signals such as which subsequent e-mails they open or click through, which website pages they return to view later, and which pieces of content they share via social media, the software can update prospects' profiles to better target the marketing messages delivered to them. It can track all of those touchpoints and use them to score the prospects' readiness for being contacted by a sales rep as a qualified lead or being sent a special offer for an e-commerce or in-store purchase.

Marketing automation software is designed to let marketers configure these automated campaigns on their own. Basic systems let marketers define a series of rules for how prospects should be categorized and engaged, typically as an ordered list of if-then statements—if *this* happens, then do *that*; otherwise do *something else*. You may have multiple *variables* of data fields, such as the prospects' geographic locations, the number of times they have visited your website, the audience segment they've been assigned to, and so on, that let you *branch* what happens based on their value.

More advanced systems let marketers design more elaborate campaign logic, often using a graphical diagramming tool, that specifies *states* that a prospect may be in—such as early-stage discovery or late-stage evaluation—and thresholds that serve as *gates* to determine when a prospect moves from one state to the next. There are also *loops* that return prospects to earlier stages if necessary.

I italicized several of the words in those last two paragraphs because they have meaning in the language of software engineering. If-else statements, variables, branches, states, gates, and loops are all programming constructs. *These marketing automation campaigns that marketers are building are essentially little software programs.*

Granted, these are very high-level programs—the top layer of that layer cake in Figure 5.1—that rely on the software below them to do the real technical work. But still, they're software programs. And the marketers who create them are, at least in a rudimentary sense, acting as software developers.

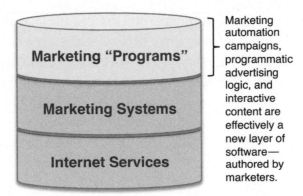

FIGURE 5.1   Marketers Are Increasingly Developing Software of Their Own

Pretty wild, eh? You or your colleagues in marketing who work with such systems are, in a very real sense, software developers—and maybe didn't even realize it.

In fact, such hands-on software development activities by marketers have proliferated over many years, as a natural outgrowth of the world becoming digital. As far back as Microsoft Excel, marketers could write little macros or scripts in their spreadsheets to customize them to their particular needs. Today, many marketing software tools have programmable features. In digital advertising, programmatic advertising software is configured with rules and parameters to automate the placement of ads across the Web and within mobile apps. Within Web experience management software—software for running more advanced websites—marketers can embed scripts on Web pages to dynamically change the content for different visitors based on logic that they specify.

More digitally comfortable marketers are even using Web-based scripting services, such as IFTTT, which is an acronym for "If this then that," to create little programs—they call them recipes—that work across multiple Internet applications.[1] For example, you could have a recipe that looks for mentions of your company in feeds from popular websites and then automatically shares those pages on your social media accounts and sends you an e-mail. It's not hard to concoct these recipes, and they can be incredibly handy. The company is working to make its software even easier to use so that more consumers, not just professionals, can build their own little lightweight software apps for tasks they want to control throughout their digital life. As of early 2015, IFTTT estimated that nearly 20 million recipes were being run each day.

From Copy to Code

Once you start looking for examples of marketers defining instructions for digital systems—in other words, authoring software—however rudimentary, either directly or indirectly, you find that software is blossoming all around us.

When you think about it, that shouldn't be surprising. After all, it *is* a digital world, and software is how we control it. Just as marketing has traditionally relied on the talent of writing compelling copy to connect with its audience, now it also depends on software code to craft digitally powered customer experiences and marketing operations.

Not everyone in marketing needs to be a great programmer—even loosely defined—just as not everyone in marketing needed to be a stellar copywriter. But effective programmatic thinking and software sensibilities increasingly need to be woven into marketing's overall DNA.

Serendipitously, this software creator mind-set leads us to some powerful new ideas for digitally native marketing management.

6

Parallel Revolutions in
Software and Marketing

Over the past few chapters, we've established the foundations of this book's premise. We've recognized that marketing is a digital profession, subject to digital dynamics, and that software controls everything digital. We've seen how marketing has therefore become a software-powered discipline, dependent on software-mediated channels to reach its audience, and that marketers are even creating plenty of software on their own now.

Connecting the dots, we arrive at a pivotal revelation: *Modern marketing management actually has a lot in common with software development management.*

That may seem a little strange at first, because for a long time marketers and software engineers were considered to be on opposite ends of the career spectrum. More than a few *Dilbert* cartoons made fun of the stereotypes of each. Many of the frustrations between marketing departments and information technology (IT) organizations in the early years of the Internet stemmed from the different and often-opposing priorities these two noble yet separate professions held. They didn't always speak the same language, and each felt the other didn't necessarily understand its worldview.

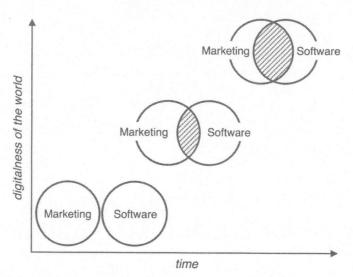

FIGURE 6.1 As the World becomes More Digital, Marketing and Software Converge

But as a consequence of the world becoming digital, these two occupations have not only collided—but also started to blend, as in Figure 6.1. IT has moved beyond managing back-office infrastructure to having greater responsibility for customer-facing systems. Marketing has moved beyond crafting communications to taking a leading role in defining customer experiences. There is considerable overlap between these two missions now. Slowly but surely, it's inspiring greater understanding and collaboration between them.

Both are digital professions. But software developers and IT professionals have one big advantage: As the world's very first digital professionals, they've been wrestling with how to manage digital dynamics for longer than most marketers have. They've pioneered a lot of ideas in digital management, figuring out what works—and what doesn't.

And this presents us marketers a wonderful opportunity. We can learn from the experience of software developers and IT, borrow ideas they've forged in the digital fire that are relevant to our own challenges today, and adapt them to suit marketing's unique characteristics.

Let's take a moment to appreciate just how much software has changed in recent history—and see whether you can anticipate some of the parallels with marketing's evolution.

Software's Twenty-First-Century Revolution

The practice of software development has evolved tremendously over the past 20 years. Most of our worst images of software development are rooted in earlier times: lengthy projects that took months or years to ever see the light of day, were difficult to change, suffered from terrible user interfaces, and were staffed by recalcitrant engineers who rejected any request that wasn't in the original spec. IT departments in most corporations had near dictatorial authority over all the software that anyone in the company could use. It was often a frustrating state of affairs—for both business users, who chafed at those constraints, and frankly, many software engineers and IT managers, who felt underappreciated in their hard work.

However, a perfect storm of several transformative changes converged in the mid-1990s and began to dramatically improve the practice of software development.

The explosion of the Internet was a huge catalyst. As the world became digital, the demand for software skyrocketed. The list of software capabilities that companies wanted grew faster—and changed faster—than ever before. The old approaches to building software, with multimonth and multiyear development cycles, couldn't keep up. So software developers began to explore new ways of managing the *process* of software creation. Management methodologies known as *agile software development* rose in popularity, emphasizing more incremental and iterative approaches to building software, over a series of shorter development cycles. Instead of sticking to rigid specifications that had to be fully planned out at the very beginning, before a single line of code was written, software was increasingly created in a more adaptive fashion.

This adaptive approach to software development was facilitated by a new model for delivering software that the Internet had enabled. In the old days, software had to be physically installed on computers from floppy disks and CD-ROMs. Deploying an update to software could be quite an ordeal, so frequent updates were frowned upon. But on the Internet, you could simply visit a website to use software right through your Web browser. Known as cloud-based software or software-as-a-service—SaaS, for short—this made it dramatically easier to use software, without installing anything. Some cloud-based software is so effortless to use that most people don't even think of it as software. For instance, Google is really just a software program for searching the Web.

SaaS broke the centralized control that IT had over the software used across a company. Although IT continued to develop and operate many systems, business users increasingly turned to external SaaS products for a wide range of software capabilities. Initially stigmatized as *shadow IT*, this practice became so widespread that IT eventually adapted to this new environment—supporting bring-your-own-device (BYOD) policies and providing more overarching governance for SaaS, rather than hands-on operational control.

This movement was the democratization of technology in business, and it connected business users and software developers more directly.

SaaS also had another major benefit: Developers could now update their software as often as they liked, without users having to do anything to install the new versions. The next time users visited that SaaS website, the new version of the software would simply be running for them—they might not even know an update occurred.

Agile software development and SaaS were mutually reinforcing concepts—each made the other more practical. Software became less about a final product release and more about a continually evolving set of capabilities. It popularized the idea of a *perpetual beta*, setting the expectation that a software program could be an ongoing work-in-progress for months or years, even while it was available for widespread use. It also led to what is known today as *continuous deployment*—a website's software may be continuously updated throughout the day, whenever developers have a new feature or a bug fix that is ready to be released. This accelerated the cadence of software development significantly, but it also made the process simpler and more robust. Instead of a small number of risky, complex, big-bet releases, software was now the sum of continuous, incremental releases that diffused risk and reduced complexity.

SaaS also provided developers much greater visibility as to how people were using their software. This inspired a more user-centric approach to creating software because it was easier to see which features were being used and for what purpose. Because new features could be rapidly deployed, developers became plugged into a closed loop of customer feedback. They could make changes and immediately observe the impact they had on real users. This encouraged them to run more tests and experiments, to empirically discover what resonated best with users. User experience (UX) design became recognized as a much more integral part of the software development process.

Software development became a front-office mission, not just a back-office one, for many companies and projects. It emerged as the engine of digital business and customer experience. And this caused software developer culture to shift dramatically toward a more marketing-savvy, customer-centric discipline. This shift was how *growth hacking*—building growth into software products—was born.

Over this same period, the practice of scaling software improved as well. Instead of big monolithic applications that grew into unmaintainable piles of spaghetti code—where all the features were entangled together, such that changing one inevitably broke another—systems were organized into collections of more independent services that were *loosely coupled* together. Each little service had a specific purpose, which it provided to other services via application programming interfaces (APIs). Each was simpler to maintain, could evolve at its own pace, and could be flexibly reused across multiple applications. Some were private, available only inside a company's network, but many became publicly available on the Internet, feeding the growth of what is called the API economy.

Being able to remix or mash up different services from different providers spurred a tremendous wave of software innovation. Small development projects could stand on the shoulders of giants by leveraging these services to build sophisticated software very quickly. *Hackathons* were an extreme incarnation of this phenomenon, where developers would compete to build software over 24 or 48 hours.

Collectively, these changes combined to transform software development from what had been a slow, monolithic process— one that was often badly disconnected from the people it was meant to serve—into an iterative and adaptive process that evolves rapidly in response to direct feedback from real users. Software developers, business owners, and end-user customers are now intertwined in a much more harmonious circle of progress.

These revolutionary changes ushered us into a golden age of software.

Marketing's Twenty-First Century Revolution

A remarkably similar transformation is under way in marketing today.

Like software, marketing used to primarily revolve around long planning cycles too. The yearly marketing plan was the epitome of this process. We'd spend months mapping out detailed specifications for everything that would be done in the year ahead. We were usually sequestered in a back room while we did that, isolated from other functions of the business—and from real customers, who were at best abstract personas on a wall. We prepared large campaigns that took months to assemble before seeing the light of day. We centrally controlled the rollouts of these campaigns and swiftly clamped down on any *shadow marketing*—anyone who strayed from our tightly scripted messaging or brand standards. Although creativity was lauded in our profession, the mechanics of marketing were actually rather regimented and dominated by top-down command.

But the Internet has disrupted that kind of marketing too.

Like software, marketing has become more democratized. It's no longer solely the domain of people who have *marketing* in their official job title. Everyone in the organization who touches a prospect or customer, directly or indirectly—which is pretty much everyone now—contributes to the marketing of the company. Everyone's words and deeds are reflected through search engines and social media. Customers and other third-party influencers now shape the narratives around our brands, without our permission. Marketing can engage with these forces, but it can't control them.

Like software, the cadence of marketing has accelerated dramatically. Detailed and rigid long-term plans are largely a fantasy. This is partly because our business environment can change so quickly, as disruptions ripple across the Internet from an ever-expanding set of adjacent competitors and influencers. But it's also because the speed and adaptability of digital life has raised expectations: People inside and outside our organizations *expect* that marketing will respond to feedback in a timely fashion.

Like software, marketing has become unwieldy to manage as a monolithic endeavor. There are too many moving parts across too many fragmented channels. Social media alone is a vast menagerie of ever-evolving touchpoints with our audience and the market, each with its own characteristics. We need to react in a timely fashion to opportunities and threats that arise in each of these different contexts—in a way that is interconnected with the rest of our organization but is also not bottlenecked by managers at the top having to serve as arbitrators for too many decisions. Neither fully independent silos nor completely centralized administration are ideal in this environment. Instead, to scale modern marketing, we want a *loosely coupled* network of capabilities that balance internal flexibility with organizational interdependencies.

Like software, marketing has shifted from revolving around a few major unveilings each year to more continuous operations. Now we have more always-on campaigns and evergreen marketing programs that organically develop over time. We still have major announcements and overarching brand positioning strategies, but now they continue to evolve after they're released.

Like software, marketing has moved much closer to real customers. Digital affords us incredible visibility into how people engage with our marketing and our company as a whole. Social media lets us directly hear what they think of us. Marketing has become more measurable—and therefore more accountable—in its impact on customers. But it's also given us greater empathy with them. Marketing has become far more attuned to customer experience across the entire buyer's journey, starting from a prospect's very first touchpoint with us. We're not just theorizing about abstract personas on the wall anymore. We're engaging with living, breathing human beings. Marketing culture increasingly champions a customer-centric worldview.

Like software, this customer centricity has combined with the adaptability of a digital canvas to encourage greater experimentation. Marketers regularly run A/B tests across tactics such as e-mail marketing, online advertising, and website landing pages to learn what resonates best with target audiences. Innovation has become one of the mantras of marketing management, as companies seek to discover new and better ways of engaging with their markets before their competitors do.

Collectively, all these factors are combining to transform marketing. Previously, it was a relatively narrowly defined function, was often not well integrated with the rest of the firm, was at arm's length from real customers, was run with a yearly or quarterly rhythm that relied on a standard set of tactics, and was generally resistant to change. Today, it is a faster-moving, more innovative engine of growth that thrives on direct customer engagement, adapts to disruption, and is strategically entwined with the entirety of the business. This has certainly made marketing more challenging—but also more impactful and rewarding.

With these revolutionary changes, we've entered a new golden age of marketing.

Two Parallel Revolutions

The parallels between these two revolutions—one in software, one in marketing—are fascinating when you compare them side by side.

They're both about shifting from rigid planning to agile adaptation.

They're both about accelerating strategic and operational tempo.

They're both about moving from a few big releases to continuously evolving customer experiences.

They're both about engaging more directly with their audience.

They're both about embracing experimentation and testing.

They're both about scaling in ways that mitigate growing complexity.

They're both about integrating more deeply with the rest of the organization.

They're both about promoting innovation as an engine of growth.

They're both about the democratization of disciplines that used to be dictatorial.

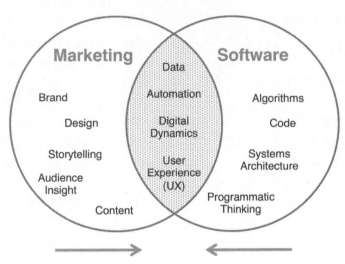

FIGURE 6.2 Increasing Overlap between the Realms of Marketing and Software

They're both about harnessing digital dynamics to their advantage.

Figure 6.2 illustrates more of this convergence. Now can you see why marketing might be able to successfully borrow management ideas from software development?

7

Adapting Ideas from Software to Marketing

We've explored some of the remarkable connections between software and marketing—and the parallel revolutions shaping both of these digital professions in surprisingly similar ways.

At this point, the notion of borrowing management concepts that emerged in the software development profession and adapting them to marketing shouldn't seem like a strange concept. Instead, it should sound like a natural source of inspiration.

With that orientation, we've reached the end of the first part of this book—and the real beginning of our journey. The next four parts of this book will look at four major facets of modern marketing management—agility, innovation, scalability, and talent—and describe a collection of software-inspired ideas to help us better harness digital dynamics in each of them.

In the part on agility, we'll adapt ideas from both agile and lean software development methodologies. These approaches to *agile marketing* were some of the first examples of cross-pollination of management concepts between the two professions, so you may have already heard of some of them. We'll dive into the principles and mechanics of transparent prioritization, rapid iterations, visualizing workflow, adaptive processes, agile team

structures, and balancing a strategic vision with operational flexibility and emergent opportunities. We'll see that the heart of
such agility is embracing change through optionality and evolutionary experimentation.

In the part on innovation, we'll explore a range of approaches to stirring breakthrough ideas and giving them the
opportunity to flourish. It's more than creativity. It's about enabling changes to the status quo in our organizations. We'll discuss prototypes and beta testing in the context of marketing and
draw upon the concept of a *minimum viable product* (MVP) many
software start-ups use. We'll look at ways of generating new ideas
and the difference between true experimentation versus optimization. We'll examine ways of building innovation into your
organization more broadly, nurturing collaborative design and
breaking out of functional silos.

In the part on scalability, we'll run through a variety of
techniques and design patterns that have been successful for
taming digital complexity in software and show how they can
apply to marketing. Some of these translate directly for managing the stack of software that marketers are dealing with these
days. But in a broader sense, these are simply mental models that
expand our toolbox of ways we can design marketing programs,
improve digitally powered processes, and govern the complexity
of a modern marketing organization.

Finally, in the part on talent, we'll look at some of the characteristics digital professionals and digital work environments
share, spanning both software and marketing today. We'll discuss
the notion of 10× engineers—why top engineers are often considered 10 times more productive than average engineers—and
how that translates to the potential of *10× marketers.* Analogous
to full-stack developers—who are fluent in multiple software
development skills, from back-end databases to front-end user
interfaces—there is also a strong case for *full-stack marketers,* hybrid contributors on marketing teams. We'll discuss how to win
the growing war for marketing talent in a digital world.

Some of these concepts might sound foreign to you at the moment, but don't worry. All of these ideas are pretty straightforward. And by learning a little bit of the language of the software community from which we're borrowing these ideas, you'll be able to find additional resources on the topics that interest you the most—and be better prepared to collaborate with your digital peers working in software development.

Pragmatic versus Dogmatic

This is not a workbook but a guide. We'll examine how these software-inspired ideas can be applied in marketing with enough detail that you will be able to put them into practice immediately. But we'll emphasize the principles over the mechanics. I believe it's much more valuable for you to internalize the concepts than to follow a recipe.

Why?

At the heart of agility and innovation is the recognition that no two companies are the same. And in the digital dynamics of today's world, even one specific company is subject to incredible pressure to evolve as its circumstances change. What works for Facebook probably won't work exactly the same way for you. What worked effectively for your own company a year ago may be the very thing that's holding you back now.

Thriving in a digital world demands the ability—and willingness—to adapt.

Our goal is to expand the set of management practices you can draw upon—different kinds of processes, frameworks, and ways of thinking that haven't traditionally been a part of marketing's repertoire—in helping your business adapt. Think of it as a larger palette, with more colors, for your marketing canvas. But it's not paint by number. Your company's masterpiece has to be an original.

This will be particularly important to keep in mind with the next part on agility. We'll be discussing agile and lean methodologies that have formal definitions. One agile methodology that we'll look at closely, called Scrum, has a very specific set of procedures that it recommends. Some ardent practitioners believe that if you deviate from those recommendations, then you're not really being agile. Some might even claim that if you don't have a certified Scrum master—yes, that's a real thing—then how can you be expected to succeed?

With all due respect to those strict agile advocates, I disagree.

Ultimately, the only thing that matters is *what works for you.* What helps you achieve the outcomes you want? What helps your team be more productive? What helps you harness digital dynamics, instead of struggling against them, in the context of *your* business? In the pursuit of those objectives, it's perfectly fine— indeed, I'd encourage you—to take pieces from different methodologies and frameworks that you like, alter them to suit your needs, and forge your own unique blend of agile management.

Be pragmatic, not dogmatic.

So as you take this whirligig tour of software-inspired management ideas, feel free to choose which ones are right for your organization. There's nothing wrong with saying, "I get this idea, but it's not right for us." Maybe it will be a better fit further down the road. Or maybe it will help inspire a different idea of your own invention.

But please bear in mind two things.

First, our default reaction to ideas that differ from what we've done in the past is often resistance, even subconsciously. But to grow, we have to throttle those mental antibodies and be willing to consider new approaches. Don't rush to conclude, "That would never work here" when the truth is "Well, we've never really tried that here." Keep an open mind.

Second, it's not enough to talk the talk. It can be tempting for companies to adopt the language of these concepts but apply them as a veneer on top of their existing ways of working (back to our natural human resistance to change). It's okay to refashion these ideas to better fit your organization. But when doing so, it's worth asking: *What exactly are you going to change about the way you operate?* What are you going to do differently in your processes, incentives, and decision making that stands to have a material impact on your business?

What will make tomorrow different from yesterday?

The fearless pursuit of answers to that question is the essence of the hacker spirit.

Agility

8

The Origins of Agile Marketing

The quest for greater agility in marketing—and, more broadly, in business as a whole—is mostly driven by the digital dynamics of *speed* and *adaptability*, as introduced in Chapter 3.

The speed of digital enables us, potentially, to act and react much more quickly to new opportunities and threats, shifting circumstances, and market feedback. And digital adaptability allows us, potentially, to alter our content and services, with digital *scale* and *precision*, with relative ease—at least in comparison to the mechanics and economics of traditional marketing.

However, the word *potentially* in those two last sentences is the catch.

It's the digital environment and digital technology—primarily software—that offers us that potential. But buying a bunch of software and plugging into the Internet doesn't inherently give you those benefits. (I joke that marketing automation software doesn't mean you simply push a button and a robot automatically does all your marketing for you.) These are simply tools. How much benefit you extract from them depends on how you use them.

For most companies, the real constraints on harnessing the power of these tools aren't the technical details of how they're used. The big bottlenecks are usually the speed and adaptability of the management layer above that. Many existing processes and organizational structures are rooted in the way the predigital world worked. They're management memes from an era when speed and adaptability were measured on an entirely different scale. Yet because of inertia, many of these legacy management approaches have been slow to change.

But looking on the bright side, this presents a great opportunity. Rethinking the way we manage marketing, to make it more responsive in this new environment, can have a significant impact on the agility of our businesses.

We'll start with a brief look at the origin of agile management practices and how they began to migrate into marketing, so you can draw upon that background. Don't worry if some of this seems a little foreign at first. The following chapters will explain how to easily apply these ideas in marketing in much more detail.

The Original Agile Manifesto

Agile is an adjective with more than one definition. The first definition in the *Oxford English Dictionary* is "able to move quickly and easily."[1]

However, the second definition for *agile* in the *Oxford English Dictionary* is "relating to or denoting a method of project management, used especially for software development, that is characterized by the division of tasks into short phases of work and frequent reassessment and adaptation of plans."

It's that second definition that we'll focus on in this part of the book. Because although it's nice to aspire to be agile—as a generic synonym of *nimble*—to actually achieve that agility requires concrete changes to the way we operate.

Agile management methods started being pioneered toward the end of the twentieth century, primarily in the software development community. That made sense, of course, because software professionals were the first group to really encounter the challenges of digital dynamics. They learned early on what it was like to wrestle with exponential changes in speed and scale, because of Moore's Law—the rule of thumb that computers double in processing power every two years. The wide recognition of software's adaptability forced them to confront the complexities of continuously changing requirements at a rate that no other discipline had faced before.

The agile software development movement really started to build momentum in 2001, when a group of agile pioneers got together and produced the "Manifesto for Agile Software Development." Without endorsing a specific agile methodology, it declared a set of beliefs about agile software development—such as the value of delivering working software that stakeholders could see and interact with, over comprehensive documentation, and the value of responding to changing circumstances and requirements, over blindly following a predetermined plan—that resonated with the larger software community.[2]

A Blossoming of Agile and Lean Methods

Multiple agile software development methodologies contributed to the values behind the Agile Manifesto, but the one that became the most popular and influential was Scrum. (The name was inspired by a term in rugby for a tight formation of players.)

The Scrum agile methodology was developed by Ken Schwaber and Jeff Sutherland,[3] two of the people behind the Agile Manifesto. It prescribed a very specific process for project management—particularly software development, although it was soon adapted for other kinds of projects—that revolved around short, iterative cycles of work called *sprints*. Scrum promoted ideas of a transparent backlog of prioritized work to be done; small, cross-functional teams that are empowered to control their planning and execution for each sprint; daily 15-minute stand-up meetings among the team; and distinct review meetings to demonstrate *what* was accomplished and retrospective meetings for the team to discuss internally *how* it was accomplished— and how they might alter their process for the next sprint.

Many of these ideas have spread far beyond the formal methods of Scrum. Odds are good that you've encountered stand-ups, backlogs, or retrospectives in your digital marketing work at some point. Although the formal methodology of Scrum has a lot of benefits to offer, many of its principles and processes have been creatively adapted and remixed into other variants of agile management. It is the basis for much of modern agile thinking in business.

Another highly influential agile management method has been Kanban. Inspired by the just-in-time scheduling system for manufacturing that Taiichi Ohno pioneered at Toyota in the 1980s,[4] David J. Anderson developed a version of Kanban for software development.[5] It emphasized visualizing workflow, limiting work in progress, pulling work along a process, and continuous, incremental improvement. There aren't prescribed roles or processes, as there are with Scrum. Rather, Kanban teams are encouraged to work within their company's existing structure and operating flow but be willing to continually adjust those processes to improve their efficiency and outcomes.

The most popular concept from Kanban is a Kanban board for visualizing workflow and work in progress. Even if you don't know it by that name, you've almost certainly seen examples, something like Figure 8.1. Picture a whiteboard, divided into columns. A very simple board would have three columns: To Do, In Progress, and Done. Tasks, commonly written on sticky notes, would be prioritized in the To Do column, moved into the In Progress column as they are taken on, and then moved to Done once they're complete. At a glance, anyone can easily tell from the board what's happening in that workflow. That transparency proves highly beneficial, for the team and other stakeholders.

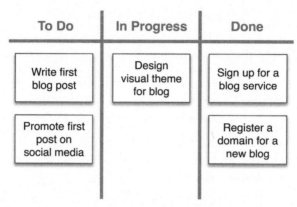

FIGURE 8.1 An Example of a Simple Kanban Board

As with Scrum, people have taken elements of Kanban and remixed them into their own customized agile management blends—effectively hacking their management processes.

In fact, there's an agile methodology known as Scrumban that is a popular hybrid of the two, developed by Corey Ladas.[6] It emphasizes short iterations that are driven by empowered teams, who pull tasks from a prioritized backlog, while enforcing strict limits on the amount of work in progress at any given stage of the workflow. Planning is done on demand, when the queue of tasks to be done becomes close to empty. A Kanban board is used to coordinate the whole process.

Kanban is really considered a lean management methodology as much as an agile one. The terms *lean* and *agile* are often used interchangeably these days, which can be confusing, but they do have slightly different meanings. Lean is mostly focused on optimizing the *efficiency* of a given process—its mantra is to eliminate waste. Agile is more focused on increasing the *speed* and *adaptability* of a project or a program, through a more iterative approach that embraces change and customer feedback. These two philosophies are quite complementary though, as hybrid methodologies such as Scrumban demonstrate.

The Lean Start-Up

Lean ideals got a big boost in awareness across the broader business community in 2011, when Eric Ries published his best-selling book, *The Lean Startup*.[7] It detailed a methodology for high-tech entrepreneurs—not just software developers but also business teams—to build products in a way that would increase their probability of success. It advocated a more iterative approach to bringing new products to market, getting customer feedback early and often, running explicit experiments on business hypotheses, and quickly adapting to what is learned in the process.

If this sounds more like an agile philosophy than a lean one—the emphasis on iterative and adaptive business development, in rapid cycles—you definitely have the gist of agile. It is lean too, however, because building products with huge investments of time and money before validating their market fit is extremely wasteful, as many of the most spectacular product launch failures in history have demonstrated. *The Lean Startup* aims to eliminate such waste, as much as we can, and avoid building things at a large scale that customers don't want or aren't willing to pay for.

It's a terrific example of the complementary melding of agile and lean thinking.

As with Scrum and Kanban, many of the concepts from *The Lean Startup* have spread beyond the methodology itself. Building a minimum viable product, or MVP, as the simplest incarnation of a product or service that can test the company's key hypotheses of what the market wants. The willingness of management to pivot to a new strategy when those hypotheses are shown to be incorrect. The embrace of A/B testing in product development—offering several versions to observe their different impact on the target audience. Validated learning from measuring the effects of tested hypotheses, to encourage data-driven decision making—rather than opinion-led decision making—in directing a product's evolution.

Despite the book's name, *The Lean Startup* isn't just for start-ups. Its approach can be adopted by larger established companies too, to become faster and nimbler in their product development. *The Lean Startup* has helped promote agile thinking in organizations of all sizes.

The Agile Marketing Movement

As agile and lean practices grew in popularity in software development in the 2000s, marketers at software companies began to take notice. Marketing was increasingly under the assault of digital dynamics too, especially in high-tech, and marketers were searching for better ways to deal with it. So it was quite natural for marketers at those companies to look over at their peers in product development, see agile management thriving there, and wonder, "Hey, could we use something like that in our department?"

A number of high-tech marketers began experimenting with adapting agile management techniques and sharing their experiences. Matt Blumberg published a blog post about agile marketing in 2006, which was one of the first uses of the term.[8] Other marketers who were early advocates included Michelle Accardi-Petersen, David Armano, John Cass, Jason Cohen, Frank Days, Jim Ewel, Jascha Kaykas-Wolff, Greg Meyer, Neil Perkin, Miguel Tam, and Mike Volpe.

In 2009, I started advising the readers of my marketing technology blog to pursue agile management techniques, particularly in support of website conversion optimization programs. I had been recently impressed by how American Greetings—which at the time was a customer of my company's marketing software—had gone from producing a few website landing pages per quarter to *hundreds* of them, rapidly experimenting with new ways of winning customers. And it struck me that such agility was far more potent than any one specific marketing tactic or best practice, especially in the ever-shifting competitive landscape of digital marketing.

The next year, I proposed adapting the original Agile Manifesto, which was written in the context of software development, to create an agile marketing manifesto, as shown in Figure 8.2.[9] Although a couple of the values were the same—*individuals and interactions over processes and tools*, and *responding to change over following a plan*—the other software-specific values didn't quite fit marketing. I suggested that agile marketing values might instead include:

Numerous small experiments over a few large bets.
Testing and data over opinions and conventions.
Intimate customer tribes over impersonal mass markets.
Engagement and transparency over official posturing.

To me, these combined the spirit of agile management with the broader transformation of marketing in a digital world. We'll explore these principles in more detail in the chapters ahead.

Relevant Original Agile Manifesto Values

Individuals and interactions over processes and tools.

Responding to change over following a plan.

Proposed Agile Marketing Manifesto Values

Many small experiments over a few large bets.

Testing and data over opinions and conventions.

Intimate customer tribes over impersonal mass markets.

Engagement and transparency over official posturing.

FIGURE 8.2   Proposed Values of an Agile Marketing Manifesto

Other marketers also proposed their own variations of agile manifestos, many of them echoing the same underlying themes. And in June of 2012, several dozen marketers gathered in San Francisco to draft a combined "Agile Marketing Manifesto" synthesized from many of these suggestions, as well as ideas *The Lean Startup* had popularized.[10]

Agile marketing officially became a thing.

Since then, the ideas and ideals of agile marketing have continued to spread and evolve organically. Practitioners mix techniques from various agile and lean methods—and improvise their own approaches, tailored to their needs. This flexible definition of agile marketing is quite agile itself.

The following chapters in this section will describe many of the common elements of agile marketing as it's practiced today—borrowing heavily from the agile and lean software methodologies that we just covered. But keep in mind that all of these ideas are malleable. You should feel free to adapt them to best suit your organization.

Such creative adaptation is the spirit of hacking marketing.

9

From Big Waterfalls to Small Sprints

To acclimate ourselves to the speed of a digital world, we must accelerate the tempo at which marketing operates. Seems obvious, right?

But the question is *how* we accelerate. The answer is not, simply, to have everyone try to work twice as hard. It's certainly not about coming into the office earlier, staying later, or giving up weekends and holidays. Companies have tried that approach, with sticks and carrots. Although it might provide a short burst of productivity, things eventually disintegrate. People get exhausted. And when they're exhausted, they do poor work, make bad decisions, get cranky, and then seek to escape the meat grinder. It ends up being more destructive than helpful.

We need a more sustainable solution. Because ideally, we don't just want to accelerate our tempo. We also want our teams to do better work, make better decisions, be happier in their jobs, and feel a genuine love for the organization that they're a part of.

Is that too much to hope for? Surprisingly, it doesn't have to be.

The answer is in recognizing that it's not the speed of *activities* individuals perform that is our bottleneck. If everyone in your company were suddenly able to type twice as fast, that wouldn't double your responsiveness in the market. Unless you're a transcription service, I doubt it would have much of an impact at all.

Our challenges with speed are at a higher level.

What we really need to accelerate is our cadence of *management*—how we determine which activities we're working on as an organization, to be able to nimbly adjust where and how we're targeting our energy. Primarily, we want faster feedback loops, with the ability to update our plans fluidly based on what we learn.

The Waterfall Model

Let's start by examining the traditional approach to project management that is known as the *waterfall model*. It was originally used to describe how software was typically developed, before the agile revolution. However, as it turns out, it also characterizes how we've historically approached marketing planning as well.

The waterfall model takes a large project and divides it into distinct stages. For a software development project, those stages would commonly be: (1) gathering requirements, (2) designing an architecture, (3) implementing the software, (4) verifying that the software fulfills the defined requirements, and (5) deploying the software into active use. It's called waterfall because there's no overlap between the stages. You don't start designing until you finish gathering requirements. You don't start implementing until you finish your design. The project cascades from one stage to the next. In a diagram, it resembles a waterfall, as in Figure 9.1.

That's how the waterfall model looks in software development. But we see a very similar pattern in how we've approached marketing management. For instance, big campaigns are often constructed in waterfall-like stages: (1) researching the market,

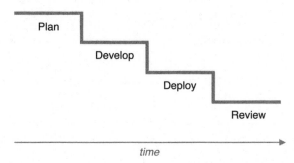

FIGURE 9.1 The General Structure of Waterfall-Style Management

(2) designing a creative concept, (3) producing the creative, (4) distributing it via media, and (5) reviewing its performance.

More generally, the iconic yearly marketing plan has followed a waterfall model too: (1) a bunch of upfront planning, (2) execution of the behind-the-scenes work to fulfill that plan, (3) deployment of that work into the market, and then (4) a review of what was accomplished at the end of the year. And then work would begin on *next* year's marketing plan.

On the surface, this probably sounds pretty logical. In software, don't you want to know the requirements before you start designing? Don't you want to know your design before you start coding? And you can't put the software into operation until the whole program is finished, right? In marketing, don't we want to have our plan before we start executing? Don't we want to make sure everything is perfect before we distribute it out into the world? It seems like common sense. And indeed, that's why the waterfall model has been so popular in business management.

The Dangers of Waterfalls

But there are a couple of fundamental flaws in the waterfall model.

The first problem is that waterfall expects us to know precisely what we want, up front, in the early stages of our planning and design. Software developers quickly ran into the folly of that assumption. They would ask clients what their requirements were, in detail. But once clients saw the resulting software, they would frequently change their mind. "Oh, now that I see it, I'd really prefer if it worked this other way."

But when you're at the bottom of the waterfall, after months of work, having to clamber back up to previously completed stages, to redesign and redevelop, is both time-consuming and demoralizing. This is why the Agile Manifesto promoted working software over comprehensive documentation. The best way to elicit people's *real* requirements is to present them incremental versions of software, early and often, and let them try it and comment on it. Authoring a massive spec up front may have a dramatic *thud* factor, but it's often more fiction than fact.

The same issue arises with waterfalls in marketing. Planning a big campaign, where a lot of design and production work precedes its release into the market, attempts to anticipate what will resonate with our audience. Defining marketing programs, in detail, for a yearly marketing plan attempts to predict what will be most effective over the next 12 months. Unfortunately, our skills of prediction are not nearly as accurate as having the benefit of seeing campaign concepts and program ideas tested in the real world, where we can adjust and adapt to the response.

The second problem is caused by the timescale on which the waterfall usually operates. Waterfall projects, from start to finish, usually have a time horizon that is measured in months or years. A big marketing campaign, from beginning to end, is typically at least a six-month venture. The yearly marketing plan is, well, a year long. Large software and information technology (IT) projects, especially back in the 1980s and 1990s, could easily span two or three years. In such long schedules, the early planning stage becomes separated from the final delivery stage by a wide expanse of time.

Over that stretch of time, things change—whether you want them to or not.

Even if you had remarkable clarity in your planning about exactly what you wanted—or what your audience would respond to, based on everything you knew about them at the moment of planning—you can't predict what will happen tomorrow. Competitors change. Technology advances. Customer expectations shift. The broader market environment evolves. And digital dynamics cause all of those disruptions to happen more frequently and spread more swiftly.

Unfortunately, the waterfall model does not adapt well to such changes. We have to suffer with an outcome that is out of sync with the market, go back to earlier stages—often throwing out work already done—or desperately try to fix things through frantic fire drills at the last minute. Those fire drills almost always devolve into "just work harder" train wrecks.

This is why the Agile Manifesto declared that responding to change is more valuable than following a plan. The waterfall model was being refuted because it was consistently mismatched to the fast-shifting reality of a digital world. A different approach was needed.

Agile Sprint Cycles

The agile methodology Scrum, which I briefly introduced in the last chapter, offers a different approach. Instead of long and strictly delineated project stages, Scrum operates through a series of *sprints*. A sprint lasts a relatively short period, possibly as little as a week, but no more than a month. Two-week and three-week sprints are common. Each sprint incorporates a slice of upfront planning, a modest block of time to produce meaningful but not large deliverables, and a review point to collect feedback from stakeholders or the market. The next sprint then begins—but informed by what was learned from the sprint that just ended.

A big project or campaign would rarely be completed in a single sprint. Instead, it would be produced through a continuous

FIGURE 9.2   The General Structure of an Agile Sprint

sequence of many sprints, one after another. Each would make incremental progress, with the benefit of being able to make adjustments along the way. Ongoing programs, such as for content marketing or demand generation, can be organized as a continuous stream of sprints, spanning the lifetime of the program.

What exactly happens in a sprint? Let's take a brief tour of the sprint process, at least how it's often practiced in marketing, as illustrated in Figure 9.2. Formal Scrum methodology in software development is a little different, but not significantly so. For marketing's needs, it's usually a bit simplified.

Sprints are about accomplishing tasks from a prioritized *backlog* of things to do. We will describe how to define and visualize tasks and their workflow in more detail in the chapters ahead. For now, just think of a task as a chunk of work that can be completed in the time frame of a single sprint. So large tasks are broken down into smaller tasks.

It's incredibly important that the tasks in the backlog be prioritized, ranked in the order in which they should be done. This makes sure that the team who will be doing the work—and all other stakeholders—agree about what's going to be worked on next. What makes this *agile* is that the backlog can be changed at any time. New tasks can be added, existing tasks can be altered or removed, and their relative priority can be shifted around.

However, at the start of a new sprint, the backlog should be updated according to current priorities before sprint planning occurs.

Sprint planning is a meeting among the team to examine the top-prioritized tasks on the backlog, estimate the work required, and commit to completing a set of them within that sprint. This is not a very long meeting. It is usually *timeboxed*—the limiting of an activity to a fixed window of time—to a maximum of two hours for each week in the sprint. So a two-week sprint would timebox planning to at most four hours; a three-week sprint, six hours.

It's worth noting that sprint planning is more *pull* than *push* in nature. The team who will be doing the work decides which tasks it will be able to complete in the sprint and *pulls* them from the backlog. Tasks aren't *pushed* on to the team by a manager saying, "You must do these 11 things." A manager can control what's on the backlog, in what ranked priority, but the team self-commits to what it will accomplish in the sprint. That can be a big shift for some organizations to embrace, and it's not unusual to see this pull principle resisted at first. But as we'll see, the pull approach is much better suited for the realities of a digital world.

After sprint planning, the production phase of the sprint begins. The vast majority of the sprint's time is allocated for the team to focus on accomplishing its committed tasks. Agile practices such as Scrum are often considered lightweight management methodologies, because they have a low ratio of administrative overhead to time spent producing real work.

When the sprint is in progress, the team meets every working day for a brief 15-minute *stand-up*. In Scrum parlance, this is called the *daily scrum*. But it's frequently referred to as a stand-up because the participants usually stand for the duration of the meeting—as a reminder to keep it timeboxed to 15 minutes. To minimize meeting coordination overhead, the stand-up is always held at the same time, in the same location, and begins strictly on time.

At the stand-up, each team member answers three questions: (1) What did I do yesterday? (2) What will I do today? and (3) Are there any impediments that may prevent me—or the team—from accomplishing our goals for the sprint? The intent of this meeting is to keep the team in sync with each other, with full transparency. Issues that could potentially derail progress are not allowed to fester in the shadows but instead are quickly brought to light. Unless there's a quick answer, however, the team doesn't attempt to resolve the problem at the stand-up but designates someone to follow up afterward.

When the sprint ends, the team conducts two closing meetings.

The first is a *sprint review.* The team and other stakeholders get together to go through what was accomplished in the sprint. In software development, this usually includes a demo. In marketing, it might include a walk-through of new content, campaign elements, or social media activities—and for digital marketing deliverables that have already been released into the wild, preliminary data about their performance. Reviews are typically timeboxed to one or two hours.

There are three objectives of the sprint review. First, give the team an opportunity to get recognition for what it achieved. Second, closely related, give more people in the company greater visibility into what marketing is doing. Modern marketing tackles a tremendous amount, even over a couple of weeks, and the rest of the company usually has limited awareness of much of it. Sprint reviews can be made open invitation for a broader set of participants—sometimes even the entire company—to help spread marketing insights and initiatives across the firm.

The third objective of the sprint review, really the most important, is to solicit feedback from stakeholders on the work that was accomplished, discuss what was learned, identify new issues, and raise ideas for what can be done next. The review almost always results in new tasks being added to the backlog—or existing ones being updated—to build upon the momentum and learning from the sprint that just ended. As we'll see in the next chapter, this is a powerful engine for inspiring iterative thinking in marketing's approach.

The second closing meeting is a *sprint retrospective*. Only the team members of the sprint participate, and it's usually time-boxed to one or two hours as well. Whereas the review focuses on *what* was done, the retrospective focuses on *how*.

The team addresses three questions: (1) What went well during this sprint? (2) What didn't go well? and (3) What could we do differently to improve the next sprint? This often includes things such as procedures and tools, as well as interactions among the team with other groups. The team may make minor changes, such as moving the time of the daily stand-up or adopting a different videoconference product. Or it may make more fundamental alternations, such as to workflow or the duration of sprints—for instance, change from three-week to two-week sprints.

Retrospectives aren't recurring postmortems, which usually have a negative connotation. On the contrary, retrospectives generally have a positive tone, because the team is empowered to make iterative and incremental changes to the way things work in the organization—to make team members' jobs better and to improve the company's performance.

One of the key benefits of retrospectives is that they bake in a management mechanism for the organization to adapt its processes continually—how it functions, not just what it produces. It disarms the "because that's the way we've always done it" excuse that stifles change.

The very end of the sprint is often marked by a small celebration, such as a happy hour or a lunch out for the team.

And then the next sprint begins.

10

Increasing Marketing's Management Metabolism

Reflecting on the previous chapter, you may be wondering, "Isn't a sprint really just a miniature waterfall?" They both start with some planning, then execute on that plan, and then review what happened. If you shrank a waterfall, and connected its end back to its beginning, making a circle instead of a staircase, wouldn't they kind of look the same?

The primary difference would seem to be scale. Waterfalls are big. Sprints are small. But is such miniaturization really significant enough to revolutionize an organization's agility?

Yes. Powerfully so.

There's more to agility than just that, of course, but accelerating the cycle speed on which marketing management operates is the foundation of becoming more agile.

Part of this agility is achieved through the *size limitations* small sprints impose. This forces marketing to work—and think—in a more incremental and iterative fashion. And part of it is achieved through the *increase in frequency*. Many more sprints can be completed in the same period as a single waterfall, as shown in Figure 10.1. For example, a dozen two-week sprints could replace a six-month waterfall-style campaign.

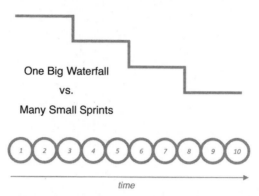

FIGURE 10.1 Within the Time Frame of One Big Waterfall, Many Agile Sprints Can Be Run

Frequency matters because the smallest meaningful unit by which marketing plans what it is doing—as a management activity—sets the tempo by which the organization moves. Not just planning an individual task, by mapping out how to do one thing. But planning across *multiple* tasks and deciding how to balance your investment of time and resources across a vast array of them. Making choices about which ones to do, how, and to what degree, based on your most up-to-date understanding of their relative priority and effectiveness.

Think of that organizational decision making tempo as your *management metabolism.*

If those kinds of explicit trade-off decisions happen only as a part of a yearly marketing plan, then you're running—well, maybe *running* isn't the right verb—at a yearly tempo. Of course, most companies today already do better than that by creating quarterly plans that adjust priorities and trade-offs every three months. But still, quarterly planning translates to a 90-day management tempo.

In the digital world, a lot can happen in 90 days.

Instead, if you manage through two-week sprints, your management metabolism quickens to 14 days—543 percent faster than a quarterly rhythm. If a competitor of yours is still slogging along at a quarterly pace, that gives you a 6× advantage over them.

Reaction Speed Isn't Agility

Just because an organization reacts quickly doesn't mean it's agile.

When something unexpected happens, good or bad, an organization can either ignore it or react to it. Even companies managed primarily by quarterly or yearly marketing plans can react quickly to an urgent problem or opportunity. Marketing is regularly bombarded by surprises that trigger such reactions. For instance, a competitor makes a new announcement, and suddenly the website needs to be updated, sales needs new materials, advertising campaigns must be revised, key influencers in social media need to be engaged, and so on.

Thanks to digital dynamics, marketing faces a weekly barrage of such issues and requests—some minor, some major—and it does its best to react to a lot of them.

But *how* does it react?

When marketing management has a relatively slow metabolism by which it plans, its reactions to unexpected issues are often hastily improvised. "Quick, drop what you're doing and jump on this!" It's a fire drill, as people scramble to address something outside of the plan.

Such improvised reactions can be fast, but they come at a cost. Team members yanked into those reactionary efforts are pulled off other work that they were in the middle of or were planning to begin. The work they were originally going to do is either pushed back—which has a ripple effect on other things that were planned behind it—or just dropped. Or, there is a heroic attempt—or demand—to squeeze everything into the same time frame by sheer force of will. The "just work harder" mantra is chanted.

This is problematic on several levels.

First, unless people have spare time—not a common phenomenon in modern marketing—trying to do more things in the same time period forces them to divide their effort into thinner slices. Mathematically, this *must* reduce the time allocated to one or more of the original tasks.

Although it's hard to measure the exact cost of that—what is the impact of trying to write an article in two hours instead of four?—it's reasonable to acknowledge that quality eventually suffers as time slices get thinner. Most marketing activities are either creative or analytical, and they benefit from a sufficient investment of mental energy.

Second, there are mental task-switching costs to dividing someone's workload into more and more slices. When people switch from one task to another, it takes time for them to reorient themselves on the task they've jumped to, remember where they left off, and try to refocus their brain. Software developers refer to this as *context switching*, which is the term for when computers swap between multiple processes—such as when you check your e-mail while downloading a large file in the background. Even though computers operate at very high speeds, such context switches are computationally expensive. They carry a lot of overhead. If you have ever tried to run too many software programs at the same time, you've probably seen how it can slow your computer down to a crawl. The same thing happens to us humans, but even more so.

And third, these improvised reactions usually do not consider the trade-offs that will be imposed on the overall organization as a result. The decision to react is made in isolation—what's our response to this immediate, new issue—often with only a haphazard recognition of how other efforts will have to be rebalanced to accommodate it.

But rebalancing happens. If we don't rebalance intentionally, it happens unintentionally. We then discover the ripple effects as we go along. Ironically, the consequences of those unexpected ripple effects can turn into new, urgent issues themselves. A vicious circle can ensue.

As marketing reacts improvisationally to more and more unexpected, urgent issues—because of both external factors and the consequences of previous improvisations—it degrades its ability to execute well-thought-out plans in an efficient and co-ordinated fashion. It becomes, as a software developer would say, "interrupt driven."

That's not agility. That's management by crisis.

Balanced Responsiveness

We can't slow down the rate at which the digital world lobs surprises our way. And many of them can't wait until next quarter before they're judiciously factored into our plans.

However, by accelerating our management metabolism to, say, two-week sprints, we can avoid having to improvise reactions, as isolated one-offs, as our only means of a timely response. Instead, when something unexpected comes up, we now have the option of saying, "We're in the middle of a sprint right now. Can this wait until our next sprint—which is less than two weeks away? That way, we can address it in our next sprint planning, in the context of other priorities."

If you're running two-week sprints, issues that arise mid-sprint will be, on average, only one week away from your next sprint planning. That's a relative short time to have to wait for a more balanced response that avoids disrupting current work in progress.

By waiting until the next sprint, the work in progress for the current sprint can continue without being diverted or derailed. This is better for the productivity of team members—as we minimize the context-switching costs that juggling causes—and it keeps marketing more *plan driven* than interrupt driven. The choice of how to respond is made in the context of the rest of the priorities in our backlog, in our next sprint planning. It leads to a more balanced response.

Now, admittedly, not everything will be able to wait.

As part of the daily stand-up, a sprint team can review a *triage board*, where issues that have arisen in the past day are posted. The team can quickly evaluate them—similar to the way that cases coming into the emergency room at a hospital are triaged to determine their severity and time sensitivity—and decide what to do, given the constraints of their existing commitments in progress.

In some cases, the team will be able to respond immediately, if the answer is something quick, or if it can be addressed with a minor adjustment to a task already in progress. Most other issues, however, will be added to the backlog, where they can be considered as part of the next sprint planning.

It's important to note that assigning an incoming issue to the backlog is *not* shrugging it off. It's not simply saying, "Sorry, we're too busy. We can't deal with that now." Adding a new idea, problem, or request to the backlog acknowledges it, gives it visibility, and lets stakeholders transparently track its consideration—but in the scheme of everything else that the team has to balance. It's not a guarantee that it will be done within a particular time frame. Other priorities may prevail. But it is given recognition and due process, so to speak.

However, sometimes incoming issues will be truly urgent. They can't be resolved with a quick answer, and they can't wait until the next sprint planning—even if that's just a few days away. Public relations and social media crises are typical examples. In such cases, the team can swap in new tasks into the current sprint. However, in contrast with the "just work harder" approach to handling interruptions, sprint rules require that other tasks be pulled out of the current sprint to make room for the new ones added. We want to rebalance our work intentionally, not accidentally. We'll discuss how to do this in more detail in an upcoming chapter on visualizing workflow.

The key is to minimize such midsprint rearrangements to instances when they are truly necessary. We can interrupt a sprint for emergencies when we must, but such disruptions are still expensive.

Instead, we want the benefits of handling most issues in a considered fashion in sprint plannings—but at the accelerated tempo of short sprint cycles.

That's balanced responsiveness.

Management Metabolism of Short Sprints

We can think of management metabolism as the rate at which an organization updates its shared mental model of the current state of the market, its options and opportunities, and what it could— and should—do, given that understanding.

Short sprints are designed to increase the refresh rate of that shared mental model.

With the close of every sprint, the sprint review gives us an opportunity to step back and evaluate our progress—not just the work we most recently completed but also how well we're tracking toward our overall strategic goals. We can reflect upon what we learned in that most recent cycle, from the performance of our own tactics to new developments in the market.

The start of every sprint then gives us a chance to act on those insights, reprioritize our backlog accordingly, and decide what the most effective way to work on our updated priorities is, given everything we've now learned.

Our plans are important but adaptable.

Each new sprint provides an opportunity to respond in a balanced manner to new events and information that arose in the previous sprint. We may not have wanted to interrupt the prior sprint for something that wasn't a true emergency, but we do want to factor those discoveries into what we do next.

EACH SPRINT BUILDS IN AN OPPORTUNITY TO

- Respond to new events and information
- Deploy viable work into the market earlier
- Adjust your approach based on feedback
- Stop wasting time on work that isn't effective
- Experiment with innovative, new ideas

time

FIGURE 10.2 Sprints Build in Frequent Opportunities for Marketing to Adapt its Strategies and Tactics

But responding to the unexpected in a timely yet measured fashion is only one example of how we can rapidly adapt our plans in each sprint cycle, as we see in Figure 10.2.

Each sprint also gives the team a short-term target for deploying work into the market sooner rather than later. In agile software development, that would typically be a new update or version of the program the team was working on. In marketing, this might be new content, new campaigns, new influencer strategies, or new marketing software created or configured. We'll discuss how to harness more incremental and iterative marketing in the next chapter, but it's the sprint rhythm that facilitates it.

Each sprint provides the team a natural inflection point at which to pause and adjust tactics based on feedback, from either internal stakeholders or external audiences. It's not that we *couldn't* have made course corrections at any point along the way before. But when we're heads down in our work, it's easy to let this slide. The regular recurrence of sprint reviews forces us to explicitly consider the question: Based on the latest input we have, how might we improve the initiatives we're pursuing? What might we do differently? How could we make them better?

11

Think Big, but Implement Incrementally

Both marketing and software development have a storied history of big projects with big releases. The big new campaign. The big new product launch. The big new website. Those big missions are a large part of what has made both professions exciting and sexy—yes, software is sexy too—the chance to make a big splash, have a big impact, and be a big success.

Big ideas are good. They inspire teams. They are bright stars by which to navigate and to guide our work. We want to dream big—to stir our imagination and to grow our business.

Agile management is *not* about displacing big dreams with small ones.

But agile management recognizes that big ideas are often best realized through a series of many small ideas. Each small idea is an opportunity to learn what works, or doesn't work, in the multitude of steps we take pursuing our big idea. We can then adjust our approach based on what we learn and readily adapt to changes in the market. We increase the probability of hitting our mark, because we are able to continuously fine-tune our aim. It's the organizational equivalent of a heat-seeking missile guidance system—a successful hit is not limited to what we originally calculated when we pulled the trigger. We can intelligently track to the target as we go along.

Agile management also recognizes that big ideas often grow out of small ones. Having the liberty to try experimental concepts on a small scale—without having to make large bets on them right at the start—lets us explore a wide range of possibilities with minimal risk. Many small bets, made across many small experiments, can lead to big discoveries.

As the Nobel Prize–winning chemist Linus Pauling famously said, "The best way to have a good idea is to have a lot of ideas."

The malleable digital world makes that exploratory philosophy practical for marketing.

It's relatively fast, cheap, and easy to experiment with both digital content—ads, e-mails, Web pages, mobile notifications, and so on—and the software-powered logic that lets us target that content to precise audience microsegments. We can update digital content and logic as often as we like, at essentially no additional cost in distribution.

That wasn't how most marketing used to operate. Production and distribution costs in the physical world created economic incentives for us mostly to make big bets on mass media for mass markets. Even direct mail, which was the closest marketing came to testing and targeting in a predigital world, was constrained by printing and postage expenses and lengthy time delays in between having an idea and being able to measure how recipients responded to it.

Even though the digital world has very different dynamics today, some legacy thinking in marketing management has still been anchored in those constraints. But we can change that.

Digital makes a more *iterative* and *incremental* approach to marketing possible. And agile management gives us the organizational framework on which to execute those possibilities. As mentioned in the last chapter, the short time window of agile sprints strongly encourages us to divide our work into bite-sized

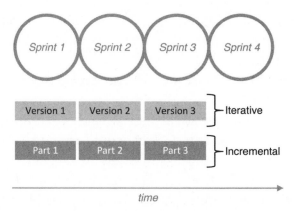

FIGURE 11.1   Sprints Can Have Both Iterative and Incremental Deliverables

increments and iterations, as shown in Figure 11.1. And that lets us tap the benefits of a faster management metabolism.

So, what's the difference between iterative and incremental? As a rule of thumb, you can think of iterations as versions and increments as parts or stages. We'll look at incremental approaches in this chapter and then iterative ones in the following chapter.

How to Develop Marketing Incrementally

An incremental approach simply implements a large idea, program, or project over a series of smaller steps.

For instance, when launching a website, you might build the initial version—your first increment—with a modest amount of content, in a small number of sections. In subsequent increments, you would then add more content, more sections, more advanced features, and so on. Over many increments, the website can grow to be quite large and sophisticated. But it starts out small and expands one manageable piece at a time.

In the philosophy of agile development, each increment should produce a viable website. Although it might be small and simple at first, and not have everything that people might want, it could be released "as is" and offer a coherent experience to visitors. It wouldn't be broken. At worst, it would be humble in its scope.

However, just because an increment *could* be released doesn't mean it has to be.

In a more conservative approach to marketing, most of the increments on such a project would remain behind closed doors. Different stakeholders in the organization would have the chance to provide feedback on each part or stage along the way. And only when the website was deemed to have been built out to a sufficient scale would it be released to the world.

There is still value to applying this incremental process, even in that environment. The website being staged should be usable at each increment, so stakeholders can actually try it out. This reflects two ideals from the original Agile Manifesto: *working software over comprehensive documentation* and *customer collaboration over contract negotiation.* Stakeholders can give more concrete and meaningful feedback on something that they can directly experience—in contrast with reviewing indirect descriptions or low-fidelity sketches of what such an experience might be.

The natural inflection points of each increment also provide frequent opportunities to make course corrections based on new information. When we determine what will be built in the next increment during sprint planning, we can factor in new priorities and updated market insights.

Most of all, each completed increment offers us the *option* to decide, "Ship it!" We can choose to release what we have to the market at the end of any sprint, if we believe circumstances favor it.

And that's just the conservative approach. A more progressive approach—one that takes greater advantage of digital dynamics—champions releasing completed increments out into the world much more aggressively. Ship it sooner rather than later. In our example of a website, each completed increment would, by default, be published immediately for public consumption.

Releasing increments more frequently like this gives us two additional benefits.

First, it provides us the opportunity to get feedback from our *real* audience. Prospects and customers can either directly tell us what they think, or at the very least, indirectly tell us by their behaviors. How long do they spend on the website? How many pages do they view? Do they share it with their social networks? Do they follow any of our calls to action, such as subscribing for e-mail updates or requesting to talk with a salesperson?

Such real-world feedback is invaluable. It moves us beyond hypothetical conversations that tend to dominate internal company discussions—what do we hypothetically *think* will resonate with our audience—and instead gives us concrete data about how our ideas *actually* resonate. We can then leverage that insight to adjust our direction in subsequent increments. We don't let our internal hypotheses stay isolated too long from the clarifying light of empirical evidence.

Second, it pushes our latest marketing ideas out into the world faster. We reach our target audience with new ideas more quickly. We accelerate our learning from the results. We jump on opportunities ahead of our competitors. We harvest the benefits sooner.

Speed matters in modern marketing, and releasing frequent increments help us harness the speed of digital to our advantage.

Objections to Incremental Marketing

Sometimes, people have an allergic reaction to this incremental approach to marketing at first.

The three most common objections are: (1) We must do big marketing efforts to have a big impact—small increments simply aren't going to be powerful enough to move the needle; (2) releasing small increments sounds suspiciously like rushing out unfinished or subpar work; or (3) some marketing programs

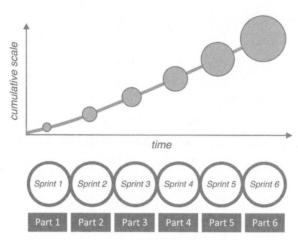

FIGURE 11.2   Incremental Marketing Achieves Cumulative Scale

simply do not lend themselves to being released incrementally—such as a trade show event or a global rebranding of the company.

For the first objection, it's important to emphasize that we can still create big marketing programs, even if we produce them incrementally, as shown in Figure 11.2. We can keep early increments behind closed doors, for only internal stakeholders to review, until we decide that they're ready to be unveiled to the outside world. And once they are unveiled, an incremental approach lets us continue to enhance and expand them as much as we want. Or, we can simply increase the scale of their distribution, in the case of advertising and other paid media campaigns or channel promotions.

Also, keep in mind that with digital dynamics, especially through social networks, even small nuggets of marketing brilliance can spread rapidly and have an outsized influence on your audience. Oreo's famous "You can still dunk in the dark"[1] tweet during Super Bowl XLVII was not big in scale, but it was huge in impact. The digital environment is ripe with opportunities for small-but-impactful marketing: social media posts, e-mails, Web pages, digital ads, and so on.

For the second objection, adopting an incremental approach does *not* mean it's okay to push poor-quality work out the door.

We still maintain quality controls on what we release, and we apply strategic judgment to decide what is sufficient in scale to have a positive impact on our market. Small can still be beautiful. That Oreo tweet and the image that was attached to it were simple, but not sloppy.

And for the third objection, it's perfectly okay to have marketing projects that don't fit an incremental release pattern as part of an overall agile marketing operation. The increments that are assembled for a single point of release—which are often equivalent to steps in a traditional Gantt chart—still get the benefits of internal reviews and the ability to leverage updated insights from the other activities being developed and reviewed during those sprints. But these kinds of long-cycle, single-big-release initiatives should be few in comparison with the many opportunities that modern marketing has for more incremental releases in the digital world.

Adopting a more incremental approach to marketing is a change for most organizations, and it's natural to have some resistance to a different way of doing things.

But in addressing objections, it also helps to acknowledge how previous approaches are no longer well suited to the current digital environment. Consider the times when a big campaign didn't pan out as hoped, where earlier real-world feedback might have been able to fix or avert it. Consider the times when a competitor snatched an opportunity first. Consider the times when good work ended up withering on a shelf because it was only one part of a much grander vision, one that never actually reached the finish line—or reached it long after the race was over.

Incremental Marketing in Practice

The software development community became so enamored of the proven benefits of incremental releases through the agile process that they even popularized a mantra and acronym for it: RERO—Release Early, Release Often.

I'm tempted to suggest we should rechristen it MEMO—Market Early, Market Often. But the emphasis really should be on *releasing* work, whether it's marketing or software, into the world.

However, how many things in marketing fit that model well?

In a digital world, the far majority, actually.

We've already described how building a website, which is a major marketing activity, naturally lends itself to incremental development. Of course, one of the reasons it's such a good fit is because creating a website is a lot like developing a software program. Steadily build out new features from one sprint to the next, continuously adding value to the Web experience for your visitors.

Indeed, most software development that marketing sponsors, such as the creation of a mobile app, will obviously be a good fit. The first release can do one thing well, and subsequent releases can build on that foundation in rapid increments, with the benefit of market feedback. Incremental development also applies to internal software projects, such as any custom data processing or integration of marketing software with the rest of the company's systems. Tackling these undertakings one increment at a time gets you base functionality sooner and allows these projects to evolve quickly around demonstrated needs.

But as you'll recall from earlier in this book, quite a few modern marketing activities are analogous to creating software. Nurturing campaigns designed in marketing automation systems can easily be built incrementally—start with a simple one-step e-mail follow-up, and then add more steps and more branches over time. Break out different nurture flows for different audience segments, one at a time. Add new additional cross-channel communications methods, such as mobile notifications or website personalization, for one demonstrated use case after another.

Search engine optimization, which could be considered a part of website development, lends itself to incrementally updating the content and architecture of your site on an ongoing basis to improve your company's ranking in search engines. Prioritize a list of recommended changes, from technical tweaks to organizational processes, and adopt them in waves.

Configuring new marketing analytics—from how data is collected to how it is reported—fits well with an incremental approach too. Because the environment in which we're collecting this information is constantly changing, as are the demands for new analytical insights requested by different stakeholders, building these capabilities out in small increments assures that we will not get bogged down in a loop of endless requirements gathering. Every sprint delivers concrete improvements to analytics that can be immediately applied.

Of course, those are tech-oriented examples, so it makes sense that they would be well served by the RERO mantra of the software profession. But what about other kinds of marketing activities?

Content marketing also works beautifully with an incremental approach. Preliminary content themes can be quickly tested in blog posts or floated in social media. The ones that resonate best can then be expanded into larger assets in increments, such as an infographic or a more polished article for industry publications. Related topics in those themes can be brainstormed, prioritized, and turned into new blog posts, audience polls, and curated collections of examples. This content can then be aggregated into larger productions, such as a webinar or an e-book.

Many kinds of digital advertising programs can be developed incrementally as well. Sponsored content and native advertising fit nicely with content marketing increments. Paid search engine marketing campaigns can be built around keyword groups that are expanded in increments—to increase the breadth of coverage to a wider audience or to develop more specialized groups and landing pages optimized for specific audience segments. Display advertising campaigns can be grown similarly, by defining additional target audiences—with their own tailored messaging—in addressable increments.

Social media marketing is also ideally suited to incremental campaigns, by being able to test ideas on a small scale and then ramp up activity around those that gain traction. This also works well for influencer marketing campaigns, where influencers can be identified and prioritized, and then each sprint pursues meaningful engagement with the next most important set from the top of the list. Social media listening capabilities can also be built out in stages.

Even event marketing programs can benefit from incremental development. New topics and audience segments can be tested with webinars and slide show posts in content marketing. Sales enablement presentations and talks given at other conferences can serve as the forerunners of marketing road shows. At each step along the way, marketing benefits from real-world feedback and the more rapid distribution of ideas into the marketplace.

These are just a few examples. As you practice looking at marketing through this lens, you will discover that the greater majority of modern marketing activities can be implemented incrementally.

12

Iteration = Continuous Testing and Experimentation

The twin engines of agility in sprints are increments and iterations.

Increments let us take a large project and build it out in stages. Each stage, or increment, provides us an opportunity for feedback and course correction. And it gives us the *option* to release it out into the world at earlier points along the way. In software, developers often refer to the outcome of any given sprint as a *potentially shippable increment*. As we saw with examples in the last chapter, marketing can apply this approach to many of its initiatives too.

Iterations are similar, in the sense that they usually start small. "What is a concrete marketing deliverable that we can produce and deploy within a single sprint?" But unlike increments, iterations are not necessarily conceived of as parts or stages of a larger production. They're either small, stand-alone deliverables or small changes made to an existing program or asset. They aren't necessarily expected to grow in size. Instead, the motivation for doing multiple iterations is less about increasing the *scale* of what is produced and more about improving its *performance*, as shown in Figure 12.1.

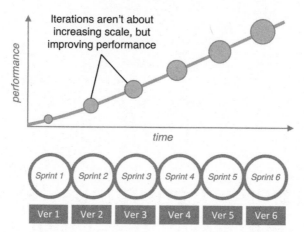

FIGURE 12.1 Iterative Marketing Aims to Achieve Cumulative Growth
in Performance

A typical example of iteration in marketing is the life cycle
of a landing page. A landing page is a Web page that is dedicated
to a particular marketing campaign—the Web page that prospects will land on when they click through from an ad, an e-mail,
or a link shared on social media. It typically has a specific call to
action that it seeks to persuade visitors to take, such as filling out
a form to download a report, signing up for a webinar, or making
an e-commerce purchase. The landing page's *conversion rate* is
the percentage of visitors who complete that call to action.

Conversion rate is one of the most common and important
metrics in digital marketing. A whole subdiscipline of marketing
known as conversion rate optimization (CRO) focuses on practices and frameworks by which you can increase conversation
rates of different kinds of marketing programs.

However, almost all the tactics of CRO revolve around the
process of iteration. You start by producing the first version of
a landing page or working with an existing page that is currently receiving that Web traffic. You then iteratively create new
versions of that page with the goal of improving its conversion
rate. These iterative versions are usually deployed as A/B tests

between the previous champion page and a new challenger, to determine which has the higher conversion rate.

From one version of a landing page to the next—one iteration to the next—the size of the landing page usually doesn't change dramatically. Instead, different versions experiment with the page's content, offer, and design to discover which variation achieves the highest conversion rate. Challengers often try alternative headlines, images, page layouts, call-to-action buttons, and so on. The page's size may grow or shrink. The measure of progress is the page's performance.

New iterations of the landing page continue to be developed and tested until conversion rate improvements level off—or other opportunities with more promise take precedent.

For many years, I worked in CRO in digital marketing, helping companies experiment with different approaches to landing pages. I observed that companies that had the greatest success shared three characteristics: (1) They were willing to test bold, new ideas, (2) they were willing to iterate multiple versions of those ideas to maximize performance and better understand *why* they worked, and (3) they were able to execute those tests quickly, with a minimum of bureaucracy or operational delays. That realization led me to appreciate the adoption of agile management methods in marketing.[1]

Many Small Bets over a Few Large Ones

We rarely know exactly what will work in marketing in advance.

We have ideas about what will work—drawn from our own experiences and intuition, learning our organization has acquired about the market, what we've seen other companies do, and inspiration that strikes us from out of the blue. But predicting with any real accuracy which of those ideas will perform best in a new and untested situation is nearly impossible. Humans and markets are too complex, and the world changes too fast.

At best, we can leverage all the information we have to make a good educated guess. But we don't know for certain until we try it and see what happens.

In the predigital world, when marketing was more limited by the number of ideas that it could try, we would make a few big bets on our best guesses and see what happened. Sometimes they paid off. Sometimes they didn't. In the days before the precision of digital measurement, we didn't necessarily know how well a marketing program performed, which maybe was a blessing.

It was high-stakes gambling. With a blindfold.

Those who repeatedly succeeded may have been true visionary geniuses. Or, as Nassim Nicholas Taleb suggested in his best-selling book *Fooled by Randomness*, more likely, they just got lucky. Out of 1,000 chief marketing officers picking a series of ad campaigns, a few will end up selecting a string of winners simply by pure randomness. They look like marketing wizards, but that may be survivorship bias. We don't fully consider all the marketers who tried all the ideas that *didn't* pan out. The wins are glorified, but ideas that fizzled fade fleetingly into the fog of marketing. A full tally might reveal that most marketing ideas haven't worked particularly well. Ouch.

How should we handle that?

Well, what if we could dramatically expand the number of ideas that marketing could try? What if the vast majority of those ideas could be tried on a small scale, quickly, at relatively little expense or risk? What if only the winning experiments were then cherry-picked to be adopted and scaled up for wider distribution?

Instead of having to guess clairvoyantly as to which of a dozen ideas will perform best with a single high-stakes bet, we can try *all* of them—each with a low-stakes bet—and then confidently select the winner. That's kind of like rigging the game, in a good way.

It's certainly a more reliable way—the hacker way—to look like a marketing genius.

The more ideas we can try, the greater probability we have of discovering winners. This is why agile marketing favors *numerous small experiments over a few big bets*. It's not that we can't or don't want to make big bets. But as often as possible, we want to leverage learning from many small bets first, to determine which big bets have the greatest likelihood of success.

The digital environment makes that technically feasible, but agile sprints make it *organizationally* feasible. The limited time window of a sprint encourages us to keep iterations small, so we can rapidly implement and test them. The sprint review provides an opportunity to analyze the performance of recent iterations, including the results of champion/challenger tests. And the next sprint planning provides an opportunity to reflect on the relative priority of trying further variations of that particular initiative or moving on to something else.

This is also why agile marketing favors *testing and data over opinions and conventions*. Because we can run small, low-risk tests, we don't have to rely on gut-level judgments to decide what the best approach is for a given marketing tactic. Instead of arguing over different opinions, the best answer becomes "Let's test it!" The resulting data reveals what the audience likes best.

This also provides a safe way to push the boundaries of legacy conventions in an organization. Faced with the seemingly impervious barriers of "We always do it this way" or "We never do it that way," agile marketers can humbly suggest, "How about we test it?" The results objectively reveal what is most effective.

Depending on the bandwidth of our team and the other tasks that we're committed to in a given sprint, we may be able to develop iterations of several initiatives in parallel in the same sprint. By keeping iterations small, we can spread more bets across a given sprint.

Sprints promote exploring many ideas through rapid iterations, but the boundaries of the sprint also prevent too many balls from being in the air at once—as shown in Figure 12.2.

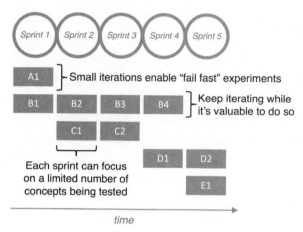

Sprint 1   Sprint 2   Sprint 3   Sprint 4   Sprint 5

A1]— Small iterations enable "fail fast" experiments

B1   B2   B3   B4]— Keep iterating while it's valuable to do so

C1   C2

Each sprint can focus on a limited number of concepts being tested

D1   D2

E1

time

FIGURE 12.2   Multiple Iterations over a Series of Agile Sprints

We'll also discuss additional ways to manage work in progress in agile sprints in the next chapter on visualizing workflow.

A Marketing Experimentation Machine

To harness the power of iterations, you want to foster a culture of experimentation within your marketing team.

Don't underestimate this. It sounds simple, but it can be a big shift for a marketing organization to make.

Traditionally, most marketing work was treated as "Do it once and be done" tasks, incentivizing marketers to perfect each deliverable before releasing it to the world. If you are going to take only one shot at something, you want it to be your best. That also dampens the appetite for taking chances on bold ideas that break with convention. It feels too risky, because there's little support for mitigating a poor outcome.

But in a digital world, we're often better off getting our ideas out into the market sooner, acquiring real-world feedback, and then adjusting based on what we learn.

Let's return to "The Hacker Way" section of Mark Zuckerberg's letter in Facebook's initial public offering filing: "Building great things means taking risks. This can be scary and prevents most companies from doing the bold things they should. However, in a world that's changing so quickly, you're guaranteed to fail if you don't take any risks. We have another saying: 'The riskiest thing is to take no risks.' We encourage everyone to make bold decisions, even if that means being wrong some of the time."[2]

Adopting an iterative approach to as many marketing initiatives as possible establishes a safety net for testing bold ideas. If a bold experiment fails in its first iteration, the risk was usually minimal. The marketing team can then learn from the experience and decide to try something else in the next iteration—or write off that initiative and move on to another priority.

But marketing management must encourage this by emphasizing three things in sprint plannings and reviews and inspiring the team to look at *everything* as an opportunity for an experiment.

First, it's good to get a first version of something out quickly, when we have the option to start small and improve it over a series of iterations. It's not "one and done." It's a seed experiment. And we are willing to iterate multiple times on those initiatives that show the most promise.

Second, as often as possible, it's good to experiment with two or more alternative versions of a deliverable in a champion/challenger or A/B test. This helps us increase the probability of finding high-performance winners and develop greater insight into what really resonates with our audience.

Third, especially in cases where we can minimize risk by limiting the distribution of our first version or running a small champion/challenger test, we should really push ourselves to try bold, new ideas. Not every iteration needs to be a wild-and-crazy concept. But a good portion of the ideas we test should strive to innovate outside the status quo.

"Location, location, location" is so twentieth century. The twenty-first century marketing mantra is "Test, test, test."

Not every experiment will succeed. It's important for management to acknowledge that expectation and assure teams that as long as experiments are executed well, testing smart and interesting ideas, it's okay for a number of them not to work out. In fact, if too few experiments fail, that should be a warning flag that not enough bold ideas are being tried.

The answers to these two questions are what matters most with iterative experiments: (1) What did we learn, and (2) how can we improve?

You can now appreciate why this book opened up with Zuckerberg's "The Hacker Way": "Hackers try to build the best services over the long term by quickly releasing and learning from smaller iterations rather than trying to get everything right all at once." That is the essence of agile marketing.

Zuckerberg followed up that statement by adding, "We have the words 'Done is better than perfect' painted on our walls to remind ourselves to always keep shipping."

Is that something you could imagine painted on the walls of your marketing department? If not, then, again, don't underestimate the cultural shift that may be required to adopt agile marketing. Experiments and iterations are a very different way of thinking.

However, as with incremental delivery in the last chapter, it's important to stress that iterations do *not* sanction sloppy work. "Done is better than perfect" doesn't mean things are done *badly*. The production quality of every iteration should still live up to your brand's values. But painting that slogan on your wall, at least figuratively, affirms a commitment to releasing your ideas out into the world with greater velocity, volume, and variety—so that you can innovate, learn, and grow faster than your competition.

Keep in mind the words of Voltaire, perhaps the world's first agile philosopher: "The perfect is the enemy of the good."

Continuous Programs and Processes

An iterative approach can work for many marketing deliverables, especially in the digital world, where we can easily run small experiments, conduct A/B tests, and deploy improvements with minimal overhead. It's ideal for innovating and refining websites, landing pages, digital advertising, e-mail marketing messages, content marketing themes, sales enablement, mobile apps, and more.

But we can also use agile sprints to iteratively improve marketing programs, processes, and practices that are larger than individual marketing assets.

One of the largest changes happening in marketing is a shift from one-off and episodic campaigns to more always on—or continuous—marketing programs. Although they have a beginning, they don't necessarily have a distinct end. They're not like traditional promotional campaigns, where a set of creatives is distributed for a limited time. Instead, these programs continuously run for prospects and customers to interact with whenever they choose.

Your website is a perfect example of a continuous marketing program. It's always open to receive visitors. You may feature different content or promotions at different times, but the overall website is continuously operating. It never ends but rather evolves over time.

Other examples of these kinds of continuous marketing programs include search engine marketing campaigns, lead-nurturing campaigns through marketing automation, social media relationship management, and subscription-oriented content marketing.

Continuous marketing programs are perfect for iterative improvement through agile sprints. Each sprint can prioritize small changes to those programs, structured as experiments to test their impact on relevant performance metrics.

The same kind of iterative thinking can also be applied to continually improve back-office marketing processes as well, such as workflows, playbooks, or procedures in marketing operations.

Iteration in agile sprints empowers marketing with an engine for evolution. It lets us approach modifications to assets, programs, and processes alike through the same lens of prioritized changes that we track and evaluate.

It's agile because we keep the size of each iteration small enough to implement it quickly and harness the benefit of feedback. But it also incorporates the essence of lean thinking: continual improvement to increase performance and reduce waste.

13

Visualizing Work and Workflow to Prevent Chaos

Short loops of incremental and iterative work, with built-in checkpoints for feedback and adaptation, are the engine of agile management. But visualizing your work and workflow establishes a framework in which that engine can run fast—yet in a controlled and efficient fashion.

As we accelerate the speed at which marketing management is operating, dividing larger projects into bite-sized increments and enabling more small-scale experiments, we increase the number of moving pieces in our field of vision. To avoid being overwhelmed—and to prevent chaos—we need a system by which we can identify and track all of these tasks, their relative size and priority, where they are in the pipeline of work being done, who's doing what, and what everyone agrees will happen next.

We'd also like that system to be easy to understand and simple to use—a lightweight process—so that it doesn't become a drag on our momentum. Sound like too much to ask for?

Three of the major agile management methodologies—Scrum, Kanban, and Scrumban—have converged on a similar mechanism for this that works really well. Sometimes called

Scrum boards or task boards, they're really all variations of a *Kanban board*.

As I briefly introduced earlier, you can picture a Kanban board as a whiteboard divided into columns. Each column represents a workflow stage that tasks move through. The simplest Kanban board typically has three columns: To Do, In Progress, and Done. Tasks are written on sticky notes, called *cards*, which move from one column to the next as they're being handled.

Even in its most basic incarnation, a Kanban board lets everyone on the team—as well as other stakeholders—see what's queued up to be done, what's currently being worked on, and what has been completed. For any given task, we can know in a glance exactly where it's at.

That's a great start. But a Kanban board can offer many more benefits.

Designing Your Own Kanban Board

The practice of Kanban, at least in the way that it's been adapted to agile management, begins with the principle of visualizing your workflow. Once everyone can see what's actually happening—sharing a view of the same objective reality—it's easier to see where bottlenecks or other difficulties may be arising. The team is encouraged to then make incremental changes to processes to improve efficiency.

Conceptually, this is a relatively straightforward thing to do. But when teams go through this exercise together, they often have many aha moments of discovery. The gaps between the *theory* of how things get done and what really happens in *practice* are quickly revealed.

Although drawing a detailed diagram of your workflow can be helpful to illustrate all the different moving parts in your group's operations—a process known as *value stream mapping* among Kanban practitioners[1]—greater benefits are achieved by designing the columns of your Kanban board to reflect that workflow and using it to guide your day-to-day work. This makes the workflow more tangible, as everyone can observe tasks moving through it.

The Kanban board can then serve as the up-to-date central reference point for the whole group. Anyone who wants to know what's happening with the team can look at the board and see for himself or herself.

It's not the prettiest of analogies, but a good Kanban board is like monitoring the team's collective digestive system for the work it consumes. We observe things moving from mouth, to stomach, to intestines, and so on—and we can see where and when things get slowed down or stopped up. Metaphorically speaking.

The challenge with Kanban boards is designing them so that they balance simplicity and accuracy. You want to represent the different stages of your workflow as columns on the board. However, you don't want to do that at such a microscopic level that you end up with dozens of unreadable columns stretched across the wall.

One approach is to think of any significant gates or gate-keepers in your workflow—such as approvals, reviews, handoffs from one person to another, or releases out into the world—and use those to define the columns of your board. Another approach is to think of parts of your workflow that have limits as to how many tasks can be in the same stage at the same time before your effectiveness in getting them all done begins to degrade.

I recommend beginning with a relatively simple Kanban board to get started and then refining it as the team becomes practiced at using it. For many teams, the basic three columns—To Do, In Progress, and Done—is a good way to get them oriented with the Kanban board process. In subsequent iterations, the In Progress column can then be split into more specific stages.

A Five-Stage Marketing Kanban Board

A slightly more detailed Kanban board would look something like Figure 13.1, which has five stages: To Do, Create, Review, Test, and Done. This pattern works well for a wide variety of marketing tasks.

The tasks taken from the backlog for the current sprint are ordered by priority in the To Do column. As team members start work on tasks, they pull them into the Create column. I like *Create* as a column label, because it serves as a reminder that everything marketing does has a creative dimension—not just the creation of content but also configuring campaigns, organizing events, pursuing public relations and social media influencers, and even generating analytical reports and visualizations.

When the creation stage is finished, tasks move to a Review stage, where they are either double-checked by a peer or reviewed by a manager for approval. As much as possible, it's good to empower the team to conduct peer reviews. It prevents managers

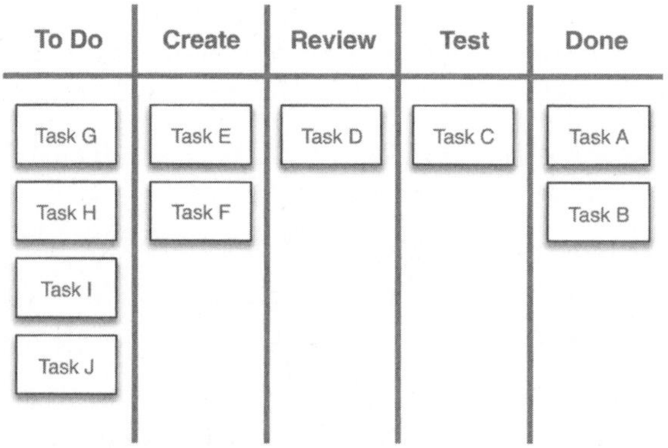

To Do	Create	Review	Test	Done
Task G	Task E	Task D	Task C	Task A
Task H	Task F			Task B
Task I				
Task J				

FIGURE 13.1   A Five-Column Kanban Board for Marketing

from becoming a bottleneck. It gives the team a greater sense of ownership and responsibility. And it distributes knowledge of different marketing activities among a broader cross-section of the team.

Once a task has passed Review, it can move to the Test stage. The Test column may not apply to every task. But in the spirit of treating marketing as a great experimentation machine, it encourages the team to think of most of its work as an opportunity to run an experiment and measure the results. An experiment might be run as an A/B test, comparing two or more variations. It might be a sequential champion/challenger test, comparing the results of a new effort with its predecessor. Or it might be a stand-alone test—let's try something new and see what the result is. The only requirement is that there is an agreed-upon metric, or metrics, by which success will be measured.

A task is considered complete within the Test stage when a meaningful measurement of the experiment's success or failure has been determined. That doesn't mean that the content or program being tested goes away at that point. In most cases, it will continue to exist out in the world or remain in active service in a marketing program. But a sufficient amount of data has been collected to draw a conclusion, even a preliminary one, about the test and contemplate what we learned from it. The task is then moved to the Done column, where it's ready to be discussed at the next sprint review.

Tasks that don't make sense to be tested can move directly from Review to Done.

The Test column in this five-stage board shows how you can use the design of your own Kanban board to shape not just the workflow but also the *thinking* of your organization. Having a Test stage on the board incentivizes everyone on the team to consider how any given task might be tested and measured. You'd have to be able to explain to the rest of the team in the sprint review why a particular task *didn't* need a test.

Limiting Work in Progress

Two other refinements to the use of a Kanban board are helpful in agile management.

The first is limiting work in progress, often abbreviated WIP. When we try to juggle too many balls in the air at one time, we pay a price for it. A Kanban board prevents a task from being lost when we interrupt it with something else—its card will still be on the board where it was last left—which is a nice safety net. However, it doesn't reduce the high switching costs of thrashing back and forth between too many tasks. It doesn't stop us from shortchanging tasks of sufficient time and mental focus to do them well. And it doesn't prevent tasks from getting delayed or stuck because they keep being displaced by others.

Kanban offers a simple but effective solution: *work in progress limits*, or WIP limits.

Each column on a Kanban board can have a limit on the maximum number of tasks that can be in that stage at one time. If a column is full, then no more tasks can be added to it until a space opens up from existing work being cleared out. This prevents half-finished work from piling up unchecked in any given stage and the many problems that stem from that.

When a given column is full and isn't moving as fast as the columns behind it, it becomes a bottleneck to the workflow. On a Kanban board, however, such bottlenecks become immediately apparent. Depending on the nature of the stage where things are backed up, other team members can then pitch in to help clear out the occupied column. Or, if that's not feasible because of dependencies on more specialized team members or external constraints, they can focus on tasks in earlier stages to fill the pipeline further upstream. This is the essence of just-in-time (JIT) manufacturing, but we can apply it to a pipeline of marketing work as well.

Recurring bottlenecks become obvious and can then be discussed in sprint retrospectives to brainstorm process improvements that will resolve them more permanently.

Variations on WIP limits can include restricting the number of tasks that any one *person* on the team can have in progress across the workflow. This is often helpful when individual team members tend to carry tasks through all the different stages themselves. They have to focus on completing their current WIP before taking on more.

Another variation, one that is a little less restrictive, simply limits that total number of tasks that can be in progress, across *all* stages of the workflow, by the entire team as a whole. That's more flexible, particularly if clusters of tasks need to flow through the pipeline together. However, it can lead to bubbles of work being backed up in any one stage if the overall flow isn't carefully monitored.

What are the right WIP limits per stage, per person, per team?

Not to be cagey, but it depends. It depends on the work, the workflow, the team, and the broader context of the rest of your company. You may also point out that not all tasks are equal in size—a topic that we'll cover in the next chapter—so WIP limits might need to consider that as well. However, these are exactly the kinds of parameters that the team is encouraged to discuss in sprint retrospectives, to make incremental adjustments to the process.

The Pull Principle

The second refinement to using a Kanban board requiring tasks to be *pulled* by the next stage ahead—rather than being *pushed* from the previous stage behind. That may sound like a subtle distinction, but it's one of the key principles of lean management.

One benefit of the pull approach is logistical. It guarantees that the next stage is ready to handle another task. This is especially important when different people are involved at different stages. It also helps if there are other constraints or setup work that needs to happen in a particular stage before another task can be accepted. For example, there is probably a limit on the number of concurrent A/B tests that can be running on your website's home page at the same time. Upcoming tasks are not allowed to interrupt those currently in progress. Instead, the next stage requests a new task when it's ready for it.

The other benefit of pull is psychological. Team members don't have work assigned to them, but instead they take the initiative to accept a new task and commit to completing it. Each task on a Kanban board should always have an owner, even if the owner changes from one stage to the next. The owner takes responsibility for the task, and because he or she proactively pulled it—instead of reacting to someone else pushing it—there is no excuse for it to slip between the cracks.

You pull only what you can commit to completing.

We'll examine more of the dynamics of agile teams in an upcoming chapter, but the pull principle is a good example of how agile management seeks to empower the individuals actually doing the work.

However, the pull principle does raise a minor process question with the Kanban board. How do you know when a task is finished in one stage and ready for the next? For instance, with our five-stage marketing board example earlier in this chapter, how does someone in the Review stage know a task is complete in the Create stage and ready to be pulled?

This can be fixed with a small change to the board, as shown in Figure 13.2, by splitting stages into two subcolumns: an in-progress subcolumn and a ready-to-proceed subcolumn. These can be separated by a dotted line, instead of a solid line, to distinguish them from boundaries between stages.

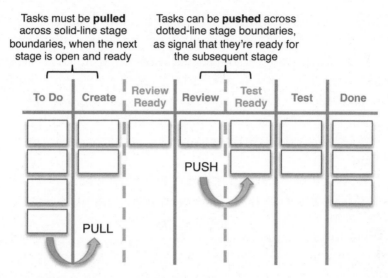

FIGURE 13.2   Kanban Encourages Pulling Tasks Instead of Pushing Them

Tasks get pulled into the in-progress subcolumn of the stage, where they stay while they're being actively worked on. Once they're complete for that stage, they get pushed—the only time a push-like maneuver is sanctioned, because it's really within the same stage—into the ready-to-proceed subcolumn. From there, the next stage can safely pull them over when it's ready.

Creative Variations of Kanban Boards

You can get as creative as you like with the design of your Kanban board and the rules by which it operates. Generally, simpler is better. But if you want it to serve as the coordination hub for your team's work and workflow—which is highly advantageous when managing in an agile environment—it should reflect your processes and principles.

Use your Kanban board as a management tool, not wall art.

In addition to customizing columns for different stages of your workflow, you can divide the board into multiple rows.

Such rows are sometimes called *swimlanes*, if tasks are required to stay in their lane. You can use rows to track tasks associated with different product groups, marketing channels, or strategic goals. Particularly if you have a large team working on a lot of tasks, this helps visualize the bigger themes and programs under which multiple activities are being executed. WIP limits can optionally be applied to different rows or to different stages within each row.

You can also create spots on your board where tasks sit outside the primary workflow. One example would be a Triage box, where issues that arise midsprint are placed for review by the team at the next daily stand-up. Triage tasks can be quickly resolved and moved to the Done column, or they can be queued into the backlog—which is usually maintained separately from the Kanban board of active work. Or, in urgent cases, triage tasks can be moved to the To Do column of the current sprint— bumping out other tasks, if necessary to make room.

Other out-of-flow boxes might include a Bumped bin for tasks that are swapped out of the current sprint to make room for something urgent and a Killed bin for tasks that have been intentionally aborted midsprint, because of shifting circumstances. The team can then examine them in the end-of-sprint review. An expanded version of the five-stage marketing board with these features added might look something like Figure 13.3.

Of course, there are near-infinite ways to customize your own Kanban board. But again, it's usually best to start simply and let the team enhance the board iteratively from sprint to sprint.

In larger marketing organizations, where you have multiple teams or several independent marketing programs, you will probably want to manage them with separate Kanban boards. That way no one board becomes unwieldy in scope. In fact, each of those boards may have a different design, tailored to the workflow of each team or program.

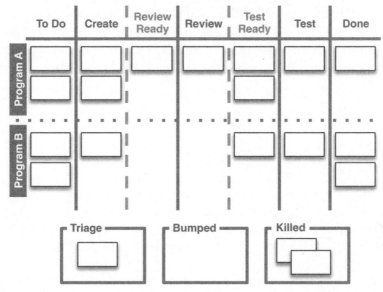

FIGURE 13.3   An Expanded Kanban Board Template for Marketing

Finally, although we've described a Kanban board as a physical object—a whiteboard with a bunch of sticky notes on it—you can also create and manage one electronically instead. There's a wide variety of software for building and maintaining Kanban boards, including many Web-based tools. A few of them are even free.

Software-powered Kanban boards offer a lot of advantages. If your team or company is distributed across multiple locations, an online board is necessary to let everyone access it. But Kanban software can also help enforce board rules, such as WIP limits and pull principles; make it easier to edit tasks without rewriting sticky notes; chart the velocity at which tasks are moving through the pipeline; and provide features for archiving and searching tasks over time.

On the other hand, if you do have everyone collocated in the same physical space, there is a certain charm to a physical board. It's often placed in a prominent location, so the team and other stakeholders who walk through the space can always glance at the current state of the sprint. And there's something satisfying about the tactile act of moving tasks cards with your hands, instead of just dragging them on the computer screen—especially when you get to move a card to the Done column.

These choices are up to you and your team as well and can evolve over time.

14

Tasks as Stories along the Buyer's Journey

We've talked about tasks, the units of work that flow across our Kanban board as we go through agile sprints. But we've defined them only as "chunks of work that can be completed in the time frame of a single sprint."

That's fine for getting started. Simply jot down tasks on sticky notes—or their electronic equivalent—however you would naturally describe them. Prioritize them, grab the top bunch of them for a sprint, and then move them along your Kanban board as you work on them.

Yet we can elevate this task traffic into a more powerful management framework.

By adding a few more characteristics to tasks—and by organizing them into meaningful clusters—we can develop a more customer-centric approach to our work and make sure that our in-the-trenches tactical efforts connect with our larger strategic goals.

Thinking in Stories, Not Tasks

One of the innovations that emerged from agile software development was the idea of *user stories*. Instead of just requesting that a feature be added to a software program—which is often described from the perspective of a developer who would implement it—team members write a brief narrative about *why* a particular user would want that feature.

These narratives, which are typically just a sentence or two, are called user stories.

The basic template for a user story is a short sentence like this: *As a USER'S ROLE, I want DESIRED FEATURE so that BENEFIT ACHIEVED.* For example, a user story for a human resources benefits system might be: "As a supervisor, I want to see all my employees' vacation requests on a single calendar screen so that I can avoid accidentally approving too many people being out of the office at the same time."

Writing user stories instead of feature requests may seem like a small change, but it can have a big impact on how developers approach their work. By picturing a specific person in the user's shoes and understanding why that person would want a certain feature, the team is able to design and implement a solution with much greater empathy for the audience's real needs. The user story serves as a compass to help with dozens of choices team members have to make along the way.

Marketing can take advantage of this same concept.

Instead of user stories—because *user* is really more of a software term—we can think of *stories along the buyer's journey*. We don't want to simply churn out marketing deliverables. "Quick, we need to publish a pricing guide!" We want to create content and experiences that genuinely speak to the needs of prospects and customers as they move along a buying decision and build a relationship with our company.

Instead of a user story, we want to think of a *customer story*.

A template for a customer story, then, would look something like this: *As a BUYER'S ROLE, I would like CONTENT OR EXPERIENCE so that BENEFIT/REASON WHY.* And an example of a customer story might be: "As a midfunnel prospect, I would like a pricing guide or interactive pricing calculator so that we can determine whether your solution will fit in our budget."

Because marketing is in the storytelling business, framing work to be done like this helps keep the protagonists of our narratives—our customers—and their motivations in clear view. And really every touchpoint that marketing has with a prospect or customer contributes to the narrative that our brand tells. So anything that affects the experiences people have with our company, from features on our website to our playbook for social media, may benefit from a customer story perspective. It takes a little practice, but we can evoke customer stories in almost all of our work.

As with user stories, the most insightful parts of customer stories are usually the who and the why. The buyer's role comes to life best when it's as specific as possible—remember the proposed agile marketing value *intimate customer tribes over impersonal mass marketing*. A buyer's role may reflect a particular audience segment or, as in our example, a stage along the buyer's journey. If you have developed buyer personas, they often make for great buyer's roles in these stories. We want to picture our audience as vividly as possible in the work we do for them.

The benefit part of the customer story—the reason why a prospect or customer wants a certain kind of content or experience—should answer the question: What is the underlying *job* that the buyer wants to *hire* that content or experience to do for him or her? "Job" and "hire" are in italics because they're usually not literal job positions but metaphors for the underlying desire (job) that the buyer would turn to (hire) the content or experience to fulfill.

This jobs-to-be-done perspective was invented by Clay Christensen, a Harvard professor who is legendary in the field of business innovation, to help companies understand the reasons why people buy their products. He shared an example of a fast-food restaurant that learned morning commuters bought milkshakes to keep themselves occupied in traffic, whereas parents bought them in the afternoon to placate their children.[1] Commuters preferred thick milkshakes, to pass the time in their cars, whereas parents preferred them less thick so that kids would finish them faster. This insight then influenced how the fast-food company marketed and sold its offerings. And it earned Christensen's jobs-to-be-done perspective the nickname "milkshake marketing."[2]

What are the jobs that your customers need to get done? And how can your marketing help?

Now, if every piece of content and every experience touchpoint that marketing creates has a customer story attached to it, that's a lot of customer stories. Pragmatically, you shouldn't spend an enormous amount of time working on any one story as a major research project. You should be able to draw upon your understanding of your audience to write these in a matter of minutes. They don't have to be perfect—they may even be hypotheses to be tested, rather than presumed facts. But they should be genuine.

The point is to attach a who and a why to as many of marketing's deliverables as we can, to bring a more customer-centric view to how they're prioritized and implemented across the entire marketing chain.

In our example of a pricing guide or interactive pricing calculator, knowing that we are targeting a midfunnel prospect as our *who* lets us assume that he or she has a basic understanding of our category but is probably still unfamiliar with many of the details of our solution. We want to speak to him or her at that level. By recognizing the prospect's *why* is about making this work within a budget, we can shape our deliverable to speak to budgeting issues; offer budget-flexible options, such as yearly or monthly payments; and link to additional content that helps make the business case for budgeting for this investment.

Of course, not everything that marketing works on is directly intended for buyers. Work in marketing operations, marketing technology, market research, marketing analytics, and other supporting functions—from generating reports to designing your software infrastructure—primarily serve people inside the organization.

The work done for these internal projects and services can benefit from being managed as stories too. It's just that the *who* is now a stakeholder inside the company, and the *why* is often a desire for better decision making or expanded marketing capabilities. But clarity on the intended audience and their real needs and motivations is valuable in these cases too, to judge their relative priority and guide their implementation.

We can call these kinds of internal stories *staff stories*, and a template for them might look like this: *As an INTERNAL ROLE, I would like CAPABILITY, DATA, ETC. so that BENEFIT/REASON WHY.* For example: "As a marketing manager, I would like A/B testing software on our website so that I can experiment with different promotions on our home page."

Stories in the Backlog, Tasks in the Sprint

These stories, both customer stories and staff stories, as shown in Figure 14.1, can serve as the primary currency of marketing's prioritized workload.

We briefly discussed in an earlier chapter how agile sprint cycles begin with updates to the backlog of work to do. Then during sprint planning, the team pulls the top-priority items from the backlog, adds them to the To Do column of that sprint's Kanban board, and proceeds to execute them according to marketing's workflow.

We can now sharpen that picture with stories in mind.

Marketing's backlog should largely consist of customer stories and staff stories. If you have a large marketing department, you may have different backlogs for different groups, just to keep any one backlog manageable in size. The granularity of stories—a specific who, what, and why—is detailed enough to support fast-paced, agile management (see Figure 14.1). But it stops short of dictating task-based steps required to fulfill those stories.

At the moment a story is pulled into a sprint from the backlog, the team, as part of its sprint planning, may translate it into multiple tasks. The general rule is that a task should be small enough to be completed within the time frame of a single sprint. It may be handled by a single team member or by a sequence of handoffs among several people.

Some stories will be small enough that they don't need to be further broken down into tasks. For instance, a customer story for a blog post or a simple e-mail campaign may already be bite sized enough to move through your Kanban board as is. However, a larger customer story, such as a big content marketing piece, might be divided into tasks for writing, graphic design,

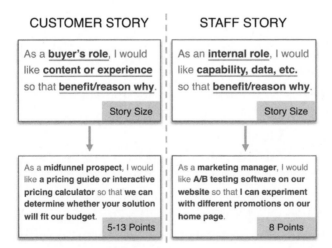

FIGURE 14.1   Sprint Planning Moves Stories from the Backlog to the Sprint and Defines the Tasks to Be Done

a landing page, an e-mail notification, social media promotion, and so on.

One consideration in divvying up a story into tasks is what work can be done in *parallel*, with multiple people working on related tasks at the same time, and what work is better done in a *serial* order, where one person starts his or her part only after another person finishes an earlier part.

Work that can be done in parallel may be divided into as many tasks as team members can productively work on at the same time. In contrast, work that is frequently done in a serial sequence may be better served by having separate columns in your Kanban board, to facilitate coordinated handoffs of a task from one team member to the next.

You have considerable flexibility when deciding how stories should be divided into tasks. If the division is too granular, your Kanban board becomes too noisy with minutia. If it's not granular enough, you lose transparency into your workflow and reduce your options for agility. In between those two poles is a wide range of possibilities, and you should adjust task granularity to suit your team and circumstances.

Choices of task granularity and parallel versus serial workflow are good topics to discuss in sprint retrospectives.

One more suggestion: When breaking stories into multiple tasks, it's a good idea to make sure that tasks always point back to the story from which they originated, so anyone working on a task can have the context of the larger *who*, *what*, and *why* motivating his or her work.

The Backlog as an Agile Management Tool

The most important rule of the backlog is to keep it prioritized.

It can be tempting to say that many things that need to get done are equally important. Trade-offs are hard to make. Unfortunately, given limited resources—particularly time—we simply cannot do everything at once. We have to make choices about what should be done first, second, third, and so on.

The adage "If you do not choose, you still have made a choice" applies. If we treat too many stories as all being equal in priority, then the order in which things are completed is left to chance. Different people on the team will make different choices affecting the outcome, but without a shared understanding of the relative rank of their objectives.

By insisting that your backlog always be prioritized, you eliminate that ambiguity. All team members and marketing stakeholders can transparently see what's at the top of the list for the next sprint—and what falls further down the line.

To prioritize your backlog, simply move around the cards with your stories and place them in the order in which they should be done.

You can rearrange your backlog at any time. Indeed, this is one of the primary ways in which marketing management exercises agility. As circumstances change the relative importance of backlogged customer and staff stories—and as new stories need to be added to the list—you shouldn't hesitate to reprioritize them accordingly.

This is the universal agile value: *responding to change over following a plan.*

Of course, that doesn't mean that decisions of how to reprioritize your backlog are easy. They can require tough choices. But by having all the stories visible in one location, with the who, what, and why of each story clearly stated, marketing management can make more informed judgments about their relative priorities. They can immediately see the ripple effects of promoting some stories up in priority, inherently bumping other stories down.

There is no silver bullet in backlog prioritization, but there is *transparency*. And that's a valuable instrument in a swiftly moving market, where you want your management trade-offs to be intentional, not accidental.

Over time, your backlog will likely grow. Usually, the rate at which new customer stories and staff stories are added outpaces the rate at which they can be pulled into sprints and completed. We often have more ideas than we have time to do them all.

This is actually a good thing.

We want to continually encourage imaginative, new suggestions for marketing and add them to our backlog. Because we can rearrange the priorities within our backlog at any time, all of our stories—existing plans and new ideas—are continuously competing with each other for their relative rankings. A brilliant, new idea that is particularly timely can immediately rocket to the front of the queue.

It is a Darwinian process, to be sure. But that's exactly what is needed to help marketing adapt quickly in a rapidly changing environment. The backlog constantly evolves.

However, to keep your backlog from getting unwieldy, you should regularly *groom* it, as some agile practitioners say. In backlog grooming, you make sure your backlog is prioritized, at least the top set of stories that are nominations for the next sprint. You also remove older stories that keep getting bumped down in priority or are superseded by new ones, a process also known as *pruning* the backlog. You can archive these trimmed stories somewhere else, if you ever need to refer to them—although that's usually rare, because new stories keep arriving.

Epics and Stories of Many Sizes

Not all stories are equal in size.

Because we are limited in how much work we can complete within a single sprint, though, it is useful to have an estimate of how a big a story is during our sprint planning. That way we only pull in what the team can reasonably expect to accomplish—for example, two larger stories or five smaller ones.

In Scrum agile management, these size estimates are usually done using *story points.* By convention, each story is assigned a point value of 1, 2, 3, 5, 8, or 13—a pattern known as the Fibonacci numbers[3]—representing the amount of effort expected to complete it. The smallest stories are allocated 1 story point—in a marketing context, a 1-point customer story might be a short blog post. A 2-point story is twice as big, a 3-point story is three times as big, and so on.

A couple of examples of stories with points are shown in Figure 14.2.

Story points are used instead of an estimated number of hours because different members of the team may take more or less time to complete the same task. An experienced expert on the team may be able to finish something in a fraction of the time it would take an intern—but the expert's time is also more valuable. The abstract notion of relative effort required for a story accommodates different ways in which the team may divvy up work during a sprint.

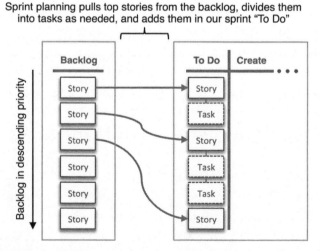

FIGURE 14.2 Templates and Examples for a Customer Story and a Staff Story

In general, story points should be treated only as approximations. It's not worth spending a lot of time precisely estimating the size of a story while it's in the backlog, because it may never end up being prioritized into a sprint. The team should offer a good guess for stories in the backlog—possibly refining those estimates, as part of backlog grooming, as stories near the top of the list and become contenders for an upcoming sprint.

When a story is ready to be pulled into a sprint, that's when the team should further hone its estimate of the effort required. This is usually a group effort during the sprint planning as part of dividing the story, if necessary, into tasks. Tasks may have different sizes too, so they may have points assigned to them as well.

Often, the size of a story can vary, as a matter of degree or extent, depending on how much time we want to spend on it. To reflect that, a story in the backlog may be assigned a range of points, rather than a specific number. In those cases, marketing management can then choose how much to invest in that story. In our pricing guide example, we may decide to do a smaller 5-point version, instead of a larger 13-point one, to be able to distribute more resources across other stories.

The total number of story points that a team is able to complete in a given sprint is known as its *velocity*. Velocity will fluctuate from sprint to sprint, because story points are approximations and many other factors can affect team productivity too. But the average velocity of the team over time should be a good benchmark of how much it can commit to accomplishing in a sprint.

Stories that would be larger than 13 points should usually be recast as *epics*. An epic then becomes a collection of stories that share a common mission. Stakeholders and the team can then see the greater relationship between those stories. Yet any one story remains limited in scope, so we can implement the epic incrementally and retain our agile options along the way.

Building a whole new website is a great example of an epic, which can consist of many stories for different sections and features of the site.

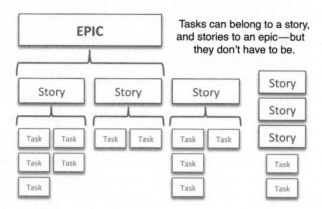

FIGURE 14.3 The Hierarchy of Epics, Stories, and Tasks

The relationship between epics, stories, and tasks is illustrated in Figure 14.3.

You can add many other enhancements to stories, such as metrics, color coding, and votes from multiple stakeholders for which stories they favor most. But it's best to start with the basics and then enhance your agile marketing story engine as you go.

15

Agile Teams and Agile Teamwork

Individuals and interactions over processes and tools: That very first value in the original Agile Manifesto goes right to the heart of agile management. In creative and intellectual pursuits, such as marketing and software development, that digital dynamics amplify, individual contributions and small-team collaborations can have an outsized impact on your business.

The hours that digital creators invest in their work are not commoditized units of time. When creators are catalyzed and inspired, encouraged to take risks, and freed from unnecessary constraints, they can produce remarkable outcomes. Agile principles and practices were founded on that belief. Empower individuals and foster productive interactions among them.

The two core principles of agile teams that drive this are *ownership* and *transparency*.

Ownership means that the team takes responsibility for what it produces—and *how*. The team commits to the deliverables it's going to complete each sprint by pulling them from the backlog. Team members are granted considerable latitude in how they work together to accomplish those commitments—often to the extent of being self-organizing. Some processes and tools may be necessarily dictated by requirements beyond the team's control, but as much as possible, the team is encouraged to develop its own approaches that it finds most effective. Retrospectives build in a recurring opportunity every sprint to reflect on that development and shape it.

Transparency means that there's full visibility—for the team and all stakeholders—into what is being produced, how, and why. The prioritized backlog and the team's Kanban board are two of the key ways we achieve this. Connecting tasks with stories helps share the context of the work with everyone participating in or observing it. Sprint reviews give a broader set of stakeholders the opportunity to learn from marketing's work and contribute their feedback and ideas. Daily stand-ups among the team keep members tightly in sync throughout the sprint. No one goes dark, working in isolation, and any discoveries or impediments that could affect the outcome of the sprint are quickly surfaced. Openness and candor are valued and embraced.

Through ownership and transparency, agile teams cultivate a strong esprit de corps.

The Size and Makeup of Agile Teams

To achieve such ownership and transparency, agile teams are relatively small—usually with an upper limit of eight to 10 people. More than that, and the overhead of keeping everyone on the team in sync becomes unwieldy, and the sense of shared ownership becomes diffuse.

Jeff Bezos, founder and chief executive officer of Amazon. com, popularized the term "two-pizza teams" for these small, agile units. If you can't feed your team with two large pizzas, then your team is too big.[1]

For smaller companies, the entire marketing department may fit into a single agile team. That is a powerful advantage, because it enables the maximum amount of harmony across everything that marketing does.

However, larger organizations can certainly take advantage of agile management too. In those cases, multiple agile teams are created under marketing's umbrella. Larger departments are usually already divided into groups—often organized by channel, product, or region—and the most natural evolution is to form agile teams within each group. For example, you may have one agile team for your website, another for your content marketing program, another for your events marketing, and so on.

But other ways to structure multiple agile teams may be more effective.

In the digital world, prospects and customers fluidly span many of the traditional silos of marketing channels and tactics—motivating our desire for cross-channel and omni-channel marketing. To rise above channel or tactical marketing silos, we can alternatively organize around audience segments or stages of the buyer's journey—such as top-of-funnel demand generation, middle-of-funnel lead nurturing, bottom-of-funnel sales enablement, and postpurchase onboarding and advocacy. A team for a particular segment or stage can then work across multiple channels and touchpoints to provide the best overall experience to that target audience.

Teams organized around a particular product or region, if they're small enough, may also be able to approach prospect and customer marketing in such a holistic manner.

Accordingly, one of the hallmarks of agile teams is that they are usually *cross-functional*. They bring together a mix of people who have different skills and backgrounds for two reasons.

First, this enables the team to be relatively self-sufficient in producing a wide range of marketing deliverables. It minimizes external dependencies—work that depends on people outside the team—that could become blocking factors in completing the sprint goals.

Second, by bringing a diverse range of perspectives together, the team develops a richer understanding of the work it's doing. Members can draw upon a greater variety of ideas to solve challenges that they encounter. Not everyone is a hammer, so not everything looks like a nail. And they can synthesize more creative solutions by cross-pollinating concepts across specialist disciplines within marketing.

Critical to making this work is the notion of *T-shaped people* on the team. T-shaped people may have specialized skills or expertise that they go deep with—the tall trunk of the *T*. But they're also interested in what the rest of the team does, and they're willing to pitch in to help with tasks beyond their specialties. They're willing and able to go broad—the wide canopy of the *T*.

For example, a graphic designer on the team would naturally take on most of the visual creation tasks in a sprint. But if he or she had time available, or if nondesigner tasks were holding up more critical stories in the sprint, he or she would be happy to help with other tasks—proofing an e-mail, verifying a new website feature, packing up a booth to be shipped to a trade show, and so on.

No one on an agile team sits around, waiting for work to be handed to him or her. As part of ownership of their results, team members proactively look for things that need doing and take the initiative to get them done. They pull tasks through the Kanban board. And their flexibility in handling many kinds of tasks, across the different stages in the workflow, means the whole team operates at a high level of utilization.

Structurally, agile teams are generally flat. There's not a lot of hierarchy among team members, at least not in the way they work together. Some team members will be more senior than others or recognized as authorities in their particular areas of expertise. But to engender ownership among everyone on the team, there's little emphasis on rank in how the group functions. Team decisions are made collectively. Agile leans toward an egalitarian philosophy.

In the official Scrum methodology software developers use, there are two special roles: a *product owner* and a *Scrum master*.

Yes, I poked a little fun at the title Scrum master in an earlier chapter. But despite the grand name, the Scrum master is *not* the boss of the team. Instead, he or she serves as a facilitator and co-ordinator of the team's processes. The product owner represents the voice of the customer in advocating for user stories and their relative priority.

In agile marketing, these roles are less distinct. There is still a need for someone to serve as the team's process facilitator, but he or she rarely adopts the Scrum master title. The product owner role also doesn't translate literally in most cases—the team isn't building a product, per se. But someone still needs to champion and prioritize customer stories and staff stories in the backlog.

Often a marketing manager or marketing executive will serve as a *marketing owner*—instead of a product owner—for managing the team's prioritized stories. It's not unusual for that same person to be the moderator of the process or process owner for the team, like a Scrum master would, although someone else on the team could wear that hat. This is illustrated in Figure 15.1.

In practice, the marketing owner is often also the supervisor of the rest of the members of the team—which is not how most software development Scrum teams are structured. In such

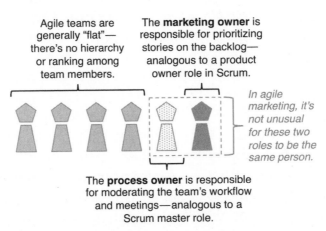

Agile teams are generally "flat"—there's no hierarchy or ranking among team members.

The **marketing owner** is responsible for prioritizing stories on the backlog—analogous to a product owner role in Scrum.

In agile marketing, it's not unusual for these two roles to be the same person.

The **process owner** is responsible for moderating the team's workflow and meetings—analogous to a Scrum master role.

FIGURE 15.1   The Flat Structure of an Agile Team

circumstances, the marketing owner should take care to not slip into boss mode, telling the team what to do, when, and how. If that happens, the rest of the team loses its sense of ownership.

Instead, a supervisor who is connected with an agile team, especially one taking on the roles of both marketing owner and process owner, may find it helpful to embrace the concept of *servant leadership*.[2] Your focus becomes doing whatever is necessary to support and enable the team, from acquiring resources to removing obstacles that hinder momentum. Instead of boss mode, think champion mode.

The Value of Distributed Leadership

Many themes of agile management emphasize distributed leadership, giving teams more independence and authority than traditional top-down organizations. But why?

There are five reasons.

First, as we already discussed, empowering teams instills a greater sense of ownership in them for the work they're doing. They're not just instructed to do activities by someone else with the plan. Instead, they're invited to apply their own imagination and critical thinking to achieve story-driven outcomes. *Managing for outcomes instead of activities* is one of the key principles of agile and lean thinking. It inspires greater creativity and entrepreneurship across the team.

Second, in a digital world, there are far too many moving parts, changing too rapidly, for managers and executives to be the deciders of everything. Top-down decision making quickly becomes a bottleneck. Organizations need more distributed decision making to keep up. The greater ownership that an agile team has imbues it with greater responsibility to make decisions, especially around process questions of *how*. This frees up executives to focus more on the *what* and the *why* at the next level up.

Third, the digital world gives individuals and small teams much more leverage than in the past. They can harness technology to produce significant outcomes without requiring large-scale coordination across as many other people. Because agile teams can operate with greater independence, organizations can increase marketing's overall throughput by loosening some controls that were previously necessary to synchronize larger production teams.

Fourth, given that leverage and increased responsibility, agile teams develop the most accurate understanding of their unique capabilities. No two teams are exactly the same. It's preferable for them to pull stories and tasks through their workflow, rather than having them pushed by a manager, because they are the closest to the daily reality of their work. They can optimize their processes more productively than most managers could.

And fifth, thanks to fast feedback from the digital world—especially social media—the front lines of marketing can be more attuned to shifts and opportunities with prospects, customers, and the market. They have the benefit of continuously observing test-and-learn experiments firsthand, in the context of pursuing customer-centric stories. They have the autonomy to make small adjustments quickly to achieve desired outcomes, accelerating the firm's reaction speed. And as larger trends are detected, they have the recurring opportunity to surface them in sprint reviews. Instead of *command and control*, agile teams are more *sense and respond*.

While marketing executives relinquish more responsibility to agile teams, they retain control over the stories in the backlog and their prioritization. They hold teams accountable for the outcomes of those stories, which are examined at every sprint review, so there's limited room for drift. This keeps teams aligned with the company's real goals and incentivizes them to perform at their best.

Transparency and Team Communication

Transparency in agile teams serves two primary purposes.

First, it helps build trust in the more distributed leadership model that agile management embraces. The team has more of a say in how it executes the work, but all other stakeholders gain more visibility into exactly what is being done and how. Agile teams are *not* black boxes, whose inner workings are shrouded in mystery. They're open and brightly lit.

Second, with individual team members applying digital leverage, more work happening in parallel, and work moving at a faster operational tempo—it's crucial for the team to stay in sync to avoid collisions. Full transparency into stories, work in progress, and process operations helps team members coordinate their efforts, without a manager having to act as an air traffic controller.

The team's Kanban board is the centerpiece of this transparency. It answers *what* is in progress and *where* it's at in the workflow. One more important piece that should be added, though, is *who*—who specifically on the team is responsible for any given task, at any point in time?

This can be solved by requiring that every task on the board have an identified owner from the moment it is pulled from the To Do column. The owner is the person on the team either doing the work or taking responsibility for coordinating others working on it, including people outside the team. The owner leads that task and can always speak accurately about its status.

A task may change owners during its lifetime. Usually, this happens either as part of an expected handoff—a task moving from one stage of the workflow on the board to another—or if a need arises to redistribute work within the team. For instance, if a team member is going to be out on vacation, someone else may pick up his or her tasks. However, such transfers of ownership should still be *pulled*, not pushed, and at no time should there be a task in flight without a definite owner.

Another key mechanism for transparency within the team is the daily stand-up meeting. Recall, this is an approximately 15-minute meeting held every working day with the entire team. It's called a stand-up because the team often stands for the duration—as an incentive to keep the meeting short. Typically the meeting is held at the same time, in the same location, to minimize administrative overhead.

Some agile teams debate whether to meet every day, every other day, or twice a week. However, I strongly advocate for a daily stand-up. It's a relatively small investment of time, and the payoff is a greater sense of connection among the team, faster reaction speeds to issues that arise, tighter feedback loops, and the transparency that more frequent communication breeds.

The format of the stand-up, as shown in Figure 15.2, is consistent every day as well. First, everyone on the team checks in by answering three questions:

1. What did I do yesterday?
2. What am I going to do today?
3. Are there any impediments in my way?

**Daily Stand-Up
Step 1: Check-In**

Everyone on the team answers three questions:

1. What did I do yesterday?
2. What am I doing today?
3. Are there any impediments in my way?

**Daily Stand-Up
Step 2: Triage**

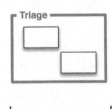

For each issue added to the Triage box on the board:

1. Resolve immediately.
2. Or add to backlog.
3. Or add to current sprint— but may need to swap other tasks out to accommodate.

FIGURE 15.2 Typical Format of a Daily Stand-Up in Agile Marketing

The first two questions are purely about transparency. The team learns who's working on what, in more detail than the cards on the Kanban board. This gives the team greater *situational awareness* of what their peers are in the middle of doing, so they can factor that into their work. It enables them to identify potential collisions, synergies, or opportunities to volunteer relevant information or assistance that they can provide each other. And if a task is taking more time than originally estimated, it becomes apparent pretty quickly across a series of stand-ups.

The third question provides transparency too, but it's also a call to action. What stands in the way—or potentially stands in the way—of a task being completed? It might be a problem with a tool, an external dependency on someone outside the team, a traffic jam on the board that's preventing tasks from being pulled forward, or a change of circumstances within a story.

The important thing is that the issue surfaces quickly. By raising impediments to the entire team as soon as they appear, we prevent them from swelling into larger, nastier surprises. The sooner a problem is identified, the sooner steps can be taken to resolve it. Or if it can't be fixed, at least find ways to mitigate its effects or reprioritize efforts toward something else.

If there isn't a quick answer to an impediment that someone can offer right away, the team's process owner or manager adds a note about it to the Triage box on the Kanban board, so it can be tracked for follow-up.

The second part of the stand-up is a quick review of any issues that are in the Triage box. In addition to impediments the team raises, this may include urgent requests from other stakeholders. For each issue in the box, the team decides on one of three courses of action:

1. Resolve the issue immediately, if someone on the team can answer it or fix it with a minimal investment of time.
2. Add the issue as a task or story to the backlog, where it can then be prioritized to be addressed in a subsequent sprint.

This is the preferred choice for new work being requested, so as not to disrupt the commitments of the current sprint that's already in progress.

3. If the issue is truly urgent—and some will be—and can't be resolved on the spot, it can be inserted into the current sprint. However, unless the work it will require is small enough that the team believes it can absorb it without risking other commitments, something else must be removed from the sprint.

The marketing owner must approve these substitutions so that everyone acknowledges the trade-off: setting one commitment aside to prioritize something else instead. Swapped-out tasks get moved to the Bumped box on the board, where they can then be picked back up for the next sprint, or if they're less important, returned to the backlog or archived.

Making these choices—what to swap in and out of a sprint, or what to postpone until a later sprint—is hard. The temptation is to want to do it all. But time and resources are finite. If we don't make intentional trade-offs, then we risk unintentional ones that could be far worse.

What makes this agile marketing process so effective is its *transparency*.

Everyone can see what is going to be bumped by adding something else midsprint. If it is worth it, then the task that is bumped out doesn't get lost—its bumped status is visible to all stakeholders, and it can be reinstated in the next sprint. However, if a new, seemingly urgent request isn't deemed worth disrupting the current sprint, it doesn't get lost either. It is acknowledged and tracked in the backlog, where it can be prioritized for a future sprint.

Transparency doesn't guarantee that everybody will always get what he or she wants. But everyone *will* always see where a request stands, relative to everything else. They are able to visualize the trade-offs. And that makes it easier for them, the team, and other stakeholders to make the best strategically balanced decisions overall.

Remote Teams Can Be Agile, Too

Because agile teams thrive through close communication and collaboration, it is ideal if the entire team is located in the same physical space. All plannings, reviews, retrospectives, and daily stand-ups can be done in person, as well as more impromptu exchanges. There's a richness to such interactions, from body language cues to physical props, such as whiteboards and print-outs. And it's easier for teams to bond, over coffee breaks or happy hours.

However, in the digital world, geographically dispersed teams and work-from-home team members are common. Agile management can still flourish under those circumstances, but it requires conscious effort to bridge the distance.

Technology can help.

Obviously, the Kanban board needs to be electronic so everyone can access it, wherever he or she is. Luckily, there are dozens of wonderful Web-based products for managing a virtual Kanban board and prioritizing your backlog. A good wiki and a standardized group file-sharing solution are also essential, to centralize team-related information and resources.

Use videoconferencing whenever possible, and invest in hardware and software to make sure it's easy to use and high quality. In addition to using video for every official sprint meeting, encourage individuals on the team to use it for other collaborations with each other. Screen sharing and Web-based, collaborative documents and spreadsheets also greatly facilitate working together from multiple locations.

E-mail is okay, but many agile teams prefer an internal chat service like Slack—something similar to Twitter but private, for inside your organization. It's more lightweight than e-mail, making it easier for team members to run questions and ideas quickly by each other. You can set up group channels for more open discussions, and even exchanges between individuals are encouraged in group channels, to give other team members ambient awareness of issues that may affect them.

Still, nothing beats time spent together in person. Remote teams should seek as many opportunities to get together face-to-face as is practical: regular monthly or quarterly meetings, an industry conference, an off-site retreat, or even just a company party.

Individuals and interactions are the electricity that powers the agile engine.

16

Balancing Strategy, Quality, and Agility

People often raise two concerns with agile management: quality and strategy. How do we make sure we're producing good work and not rushing stuff half-baked out the door? And how do we connect fast-moving agile sprints with a larger strategy so we achieve longer-term goals and don't run aimlessly at high speed?

Waterfall-style planning and top-down management were designed to dictate strategy and enforce quality. Although those traditional approaches struggle to keep pace with the digital world, does becoming more agile resign us to less strategic focus and fewer quality assurances?

Definitely not.

Agile marketing does not impede a company's ability to have quality control or strategic focus. Although it is a different approach to managing the *execution* of strategy—and a way of making strategy more *adaptable*—agile management still values strong strategic leadership. Its purpose is actually to make it easier for a company to act strategically in today's environment.

Before we discuss the interplay between strategy and agility, though, let's address quality.

Quality Control in Agile Marketing

Agile is *not* quick and dirty. It produces things quickly, but it does so by emphasizing iterative and incremental deliverables and letting the team focus on a clear set of priorities in each sprint. The output of any given iteration or increment may be small, but there should be no compromise in quality. Small can be beautiful.

Quality is enforced in agile marketing in several ways.

First, there is the definition of *done*. For a task to be moved over to the Done column of the team's Kanban board—or, for that matter, to any other column that indicates the task is ready for an important handoff or release out into the world—the work must meet all criteria the organization requires.

This typically includes adherence to brand standards and company policies, verification that anything functional about the deliverable was tested, and appraisal that the work lives up to the brand's image and values. These rules are established outside the agile process, but they remain in force in agile execution.

These requirements can be self-enforced in good faith—with "Trust but verify" oversight—or the process can formally integrate peer review or approval by a manager or the marketing owner. Formal confirmation is best implemented by having a Review or Approve stage column on your Kanban board so it is officially tracked in the workflow.

Peer review has several advantages over manager approval. It prevents the manager from becoming a bottleneck. Anyone on the team can pull a task for review to optimize throughput. It helps team members better understand the work their colleagues are doing. It's an opportunity to learn new skills and tactics from each other, as well as to see more deeply the interconnections between tasks and stories. It gives the team more responsibility and therefore more ownership.

Many agile software development teams rely on peer review for these reasons. A team member other than the programmer who implemented a given task must verify that it works as expected. Independent verifications and code reviews are considered so valuable in software development that some agile software methodologies, such as Extreme Programming or XP,[1] take the concept to an extreme—hence the name—by instituting *pair programming*. A pair of engineers work side by side throughout the entire development process, jointly designing, coding, and reviewing. This has been shown to reduce defects, and thereby improve quality, by 15 percent.[2]

It may be worth considering *pair marketing* for certain kinds of marketing tasks too.

The second way that agile marketing enforces quality is through sprint reviews. At the end of each sprint, which may be as frequent as every week or two, the team and the marketing owner, as well as other stakeholders, walk through everything that was accomplished. The *quality* of what was produced is evaluated and discussed as part of the feedback to the team. This can lead to new rules or norms for work moving forward. If processes for quality control need to be adjusted, the team can take that up as part of the retrospective immediately after the review.

Agile teams tend to take great pride in their sprint reviews and the recognition that they receive through them, which in itself is a strong motivation for doing quality work. Marketing owners should play into that by making a big deal of sprint reviews and celebrating their outcomes.

The third lever for quality control in agile marketing is the choice that marketing owners and teams can make *not* to release a particular increment or iteration out into the world. During an internal review, they may decide that further iterations are necessary to achieve a higher level of quality. That should not be seen as a failure but a natural and normal part of the agile process. Increments and iterations are powerful because they offer an *option*, not a requirement, to ship at earlier points in development.

Yet keep in mind Facebook's adage in "The Hacker Way": "Done is better than perfect." That's not an invitation to sloppiness—refer to the importance of the definition of *done*. But it is often more beneficial to get work that is good enough out into the market—to keep pace with life's digital tempo and acquire feedback from real prospects and customers—than to hold something back too long, in a Quixotic quest for perfection, that ends up missing a window of opportunity.

Beyond explicit quality control mechanisms, however, agile marketing facilitates higher-quality outcomes through its overarching philosophy. Small increments and iterations are easier to proof and validate than big, massive productions that must come together in synchrony all at once. The clarity of prioritized tasks for a given sprint, with a minimum of interrupt-driven fire drills, lets agile team members focus more intently, with fewer distractions, on the work they're doing. The transparency and ownership of tasks and stories reduces the risk of something falling between the cracks.

But most of all, agile marketing promotes quality by tightening the loop between strategy and execution. To riff on a famous quote by management guru Peter F. Drucker: *Quality isn't just doing the thing right—it's doing the right thing.*

Strategy Drives Agile Sprints

Agile management relies on strategy and vision to succeed.

Picture agile sprints as the spinning of a bicycle wheel. Each revolution of the wheel moves the bicycle forward. But strategy is applied with the handlebars, pointing the bicycle in the right direction. Pedaling (execution) and steering (strategy) work together to get us to our destination (vision).

Agile sprints don't create strategy. They offer flexibility in the execution of a strategy and provide real-world feedback to influence the evolution of that strategy. But the strategy itself must be established at a level *above* the sprints. We'll discuss how

FIGURE 16.1 Points for Strategic Influence in Agile Sprints

to develop and adapt strategy to take full advantage of agile marketing's sense-and-respond feedback loops, but first, let's look at how strategy is applied to steer agile sprints effectively, at the points identified in Figure 16.1.

First, the prioritized backlog of stories is the most operational incarnation of a company's strategy. From this ordered list the agile team pulls the top stories into sprints. So what is in the backlog—and what order it's in—determines where the team will invest its effort. If the backlog accurately reflects the company's strategy, then the team will execute strategically.

This puts responsibility on the marketing owner to keep the backlog prioritized. That's not an easy job. You can't point at an unsorted pile of stories and simply say, "These are all the things we need to get done." You must rank them—what comes first, second, third, and so on, in relative importance—according to your strategy. You can adjust that ranking at any time, as circumstances change, but at the start of each sprint, the top of the backlog must be prioritized.

As AG Lafley, the former chief executive officer of Procter & Gamble, and Roger L. Martin, dean of Rotman School of Management, stated up front in their best-selling book *Playing to Win: How Strategy Really Works*, "Strategy is choice."[3] Because there is always more we want done than time or resources to do it all, prioritization embodies our actual strategy through the choices we make of what should be done, and when, relative to everything else.

Second, by working with stories that describe who, what, and why—not merely tasks to be done absent of context—agile teams are able to better understand the strategic motivations behind those priorities. They can leverage that insight for the myriad of microchoices they make when translating stories into tasks during sprint planning and executing them with creative inspiration in the sprint. Well-written stories push strategic thinking deeper into the front lines of marketing.

It's like the slogan "Think globally, act locally." Agile teams see the bigger picture.

This also requires the marketing owner to write meaningful stories and to compel other contributors of stories to do the same. But that is beneficial in its own right, because it forces intentional reflection on how a given idea or request connects to the company's strategic goals.

Third, sprint reviews provide a recurring opportunity for the marketing owner and other stakeholders to evaluate the team's accomplishments through the lens of their strategic objectives. Some teams may even divide their Kanban board into swim lanes—horizontal rows—aligned to strategic themes, to better visualize progress of stories and tasks in each of them.

The sprint review is an ideal time for the marketing owner to make decisions about whether to invest in subsequent increments or iterations of stories or to take them as is and move on to other priorities. Learning from experiments conducted within the sprint will often result in the reprioritization of stories within the backlog or new stories being added. All of these choices let marketing owners judiciously impart strategic course corrections to the team.

But possibly the most important mechanism for strategic focus in agile marketing is the sheltered time when the sprint is in progress. Once the team is committed to a sprint plan, and off and running, every effort is made to minimize midsprint interruptions. The default answer to incoming requests, at least those that are nontrivial, is "Add it to the backlog, and we will look at tackling it in the *next* sprint."

With short sprints, that's not long to wait. But this has two strategic advantages.

First, it lets the team concentrate on the stories that were selected for the current sprint. Those stories were chosen by the marketing owner, through strategic reflection, to be the most important priorities for the business at this time. By averting distractions that aren't absolutely necessary, the team stays focused on achieving those planned objectives. It has quality time for the work, to do it right, not rushed.

And second, those incoming requests that are added to the backlog as nominations for a future sprint are not addressed in isolation. It's easy to say that a given request is a good idea on its own. But given limited resources, the real question is how that request should be prioritized *relative to all the other good ideas that marketing wants to execute*. By postponing the evaluation of a new request until it can be considered in the context of the rest of the backlog, the marketing owner is better able to prioritize it according to its strategic value. Fewer decisions are made in the heat of the moment.

Truly urgent issues can be permitted to override a sprint plan, of course, when they are absolutely necessary. But they are exceptions, rather than the rule. By default, the planned stories take precedence.

The combination of these strategic levers in agile management—prioritization, context, regular reviews, and focus—tends to make agile sprints *more* connected with strategy, not less.

Agile Strategy above the Sprints

We've seen how strategy can govern a sprint. But how is strategy defined and managed at the level above sprints? And how do we make our strategies agile, not just our implementations?

One way to do this is to picture several layers at which the organization decides what it is going to do. We've already seen two layers. The *tasks* on an agile team's Kanban board are the bottom layer, describing very specific activities that individuals execute in the scope of a sprint. Those tasks are derived from the prioritized backlog of *stories*, which is the layer immediately above the sprint.

I briefly mentioned that clusters of related stories could be grouped into *epics*, which constitute the next layer up. And we can even envision a layer above that, a collection of *themes* that represent the highest level of strategic initiatives that the company wants to pursue. This is illustrated in Figure 16.2.

FIGURE 16.2 Strategic Buckets in Agile Marketing

At the very top is the company's overarching *vision*, a layer that encompasses everything.

These layers are distinguished from one an other by their granularity and their timescale. Tasks are the most atomic units, things such as "graphic design of infographic." Themes are big, high-level thrusts, such as "establish presence in the Asia/Pacific region." An epic under that theme might be "launch Asia/Pacific content marketing program." And a story under that epic might be "produce infographic of important regional trends"—of which our task example is one slice.

The different timescales on which these layers operate are approximately tasks in a sprint, stories in a quarter, epics on a half-year horizon, and themes for the year. This coincides with the concept of long-term planning buckets in Scrumban—which, as you may recall, is an agile/lean methodology that blends elements of Scrum and Kanban. Scrumban recommends a three-month bucket, a six-month bucket, and a 12-month bucket.

Each of these layers can have a process that is analogous to a sprint cycle, with planning and review meetings and frequent check-ins among the key participants at that level. Although there usually isn't any workflow being managed in these strategic layers—so a Kanban board isn't really needed for each—it's important to have these stories, epics, and themes written and tracked on some kind of board, physical or electronic.

The backlog is essentially the board of stories being considered within the scope of the next three months. As I've repeatedly emphasized, it's extremely important to have the stories on that board ranked in order of priority, because the top of that list feeds directly into sprints.

The six-month and 12-month boards may not need to be as strictly prioritized, because several epics and themes often run in parallel and may even be distributed across multiple agile teams. However, ranking them in general order of priority—or, alternatively, mapping them along an approximate time line—creates a valuable artifact: a *marketing road map*.

This marketing road map, analogous to a product road map in software development, can serve as the successor to the classic marketing plan. Themes and epics define marketing's strategic plans with enough detail to allocate required resources and to coordinate efforts across the rest of the organization. But they leave enough white space in how stories are crafted and tasks are implemented to empower the teams who are closer to the ground to embrace ownership of their work and to adapt to fast-changing circumstances within that strategic framework.

However, it's important that the relationships up and down these strategic layers are apparent to everyone involved, especially the agile teams working at the sprint level. The marketing road map of themes and epics should be widely shared within the organization, to promote greater alignment and ownership.

Transparency across the entire strategy chain—from themes to epics to stories to tasks and how they connect to one other—gives agile teams a deeper understanding of how their efforts contribute to the firm's strategic objectives. That increases the strategic clarity they can bring to their work. And it gives senior management the ability to peer into the stories that reveal the ground truth of their strategic initiatives at any time. That increases their capabilities for executive sense making within continuously shifting markets.

The connections across these layers should be two-way. From top to bottom, strategic priorities are pulled into the operational layers below. But as results from stories are observed—especially from experiments and A/B tests conducted within those stories that discover what resonates best and why—those insights should ripple from the bottom back up, to inform and affect strategy and the road map.

This makes all of these layers fluid and flexible, in proportion to their strategic level. Stories can be added, edited, and reprioritized with relative ease in the backlog, the three-month horizon bucket. Epics and themes in the higher-level six-month and 12-month horizon buckets change less frequently—they *should*

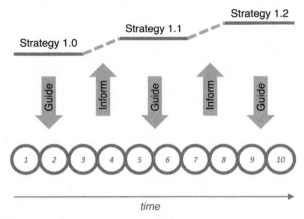

FIGURE 16.3 Agile Marketing Enables an Evolutionary Approach to Strategy

be stabler—but they still do evolve. Such evolution may include reprioritization, redistribution of relative investment, revisions to accompanying narratives, updates to associated metrics and performance goals, and introduction of new epics and themes.

These evolutionary changes to your strategy don't have to tie to quarterly or yearly planning boundaries. Every sprint review provides a logical opportunity to assess the state of the market and how you're engaging with it. Urgent concerns that arise within a sprint, or emergent patterns that reveal themselves across multiple sprints, can be bubbled up to the executives who own the relevant epics and themes. This is illustrated in Figure 16.3.

Executives then have the *option* to make adjustments at the appropriate strategic level.

Your strategy can steadily adapt in the world of digital dynamics, harnessing the spirit of incremental and iterative thinking, rather than being an isolated process that is stuck in a yearly cadence.

Agile strategy is a harmonious balance of top-down leadership and bottom-up market intelligence.

17

Adapting Processes, Not Just Productions

Agility is the heart of hacking marketing. If you're willing and able to explore and adapt, with the right balance of speed and strategy, you can turn digital dynamics to your advantage.

As we close this section, it's important to recognize that such exploration and adaptation aren't limited just to *what* we produce in marketing. They apply to *how* we produce our work as well. Both agile and lean management methodologies encourage continuous improvement of the processes and practices that teams use.

Retrospectives to Continually Improve *How*

In Scrum-style agile sprints, a *sprint retrospective* meeting is conducted among the team at the end of every sprint, expressly for evaluating and refining its process.

Official Scrum practice recommends that this meeting be limited only to team members and the Scrum master or process owner. The product owner or marketing owner, as well as other stakeholders, do not participate, so as to create an atmosphere for completely open and candid self-reflection among the team.

Because, in agile marketing, the process owner and marketing owner roles frequently blend into the team's manager—who is often an active contributor in the workflow as well—it's common to have that person join the retrospective too. But in those instances, he or she should take great care not to overshadow the conversation with his or her opinion as the boss. The retrospective is a crucial opportunity for the team to cultivate ownership of its process and practices. The marketing owner needs to give the team room to do that.

In the retrospective, the team usually discusses three questions:

1. What went well during this last sprint?
2. What didn't go well during this last sprint?
3. What should we do differently in the next sprint?

The first question starts the discussion out on a positive note. It's important for the team to acknowledge what's working well, both to reinforce those practices and to make sure that the retrospective doesn't become a defensive or negative experience. Especially if new process ideas were introduced in this sprint, and they were successful, it's good to close the loop and confirm their adoption more permanently. "Let's keep doing this."

The second question encourages the team to examine issues that it found difficult or frustrating in the sprint. However, the concerns that are raised should focus on processes, tools, practices, policies, external factors, and outcomes. It shouldn't be about blaming individuals or finger-pointing, because that triggers defensiveness and sows disharmony in the team. Instead, every effort should be made to make the team comfortable in openly self-critiquing the sprint together, with the intent of collectively improving productivity and happiness.

The third question moves the team to action. Given the concerns that were raised with the previous question, what could be done differently in the next sprint to prevent or mitigate those issues? Not every difficulty encountered will necessitate a change, especially if it seems unlikely to reoccur. But for more persistent problems, the team should brainstorm adjustments it could make to resolve them. In the absence of any specific issues to be fixed, this brainstorming can be more open-ended, to explore suggestions for increasing performance or efficiency.

It's helpful for the team to write down the answers to these three questions. Sticky notes posted up on a board are a good approach, although software can be more convenient, especially if team members aren't all in the same physical location. This lets the group visualize all the feedback, identify clusters of similar thoughts, riff on each other's ideas, and vote up suggestions they like. The structure of this retrospective board can look something like Figure 17.1.

Writing these ideas down also produces concrete artifacts from the retrospective. For the feedback on what went well— or not so well—it's useful to be able to view that history across

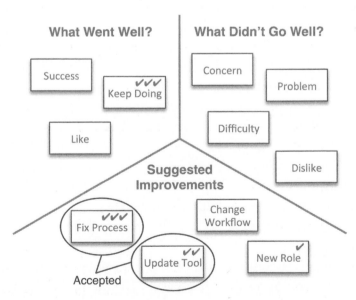

FIGURE 17.1 Structure of an Agile Sprint Retrospective Board

multiple sprints, to identify patterns of recurring issues. And the suggestions for improvements that the team decides to implement become a tangible set of action items for team members to take away.

Suggested improvements can cover any aspect of *how* the team works: workflow stages, handoff protocols, designated roles and responsibilities, policies, standards, best practices, the definition of *done* for different kinds of deliverables, meeting topics and formats, new tools, training, team culture, and so on.

It may be something as simple as changing the time of day that the daily stand-up is held or the choice of video-conference software used to connect with remote team members. Or it can be a more substantial change, such as a better process for coordinating with an outside agency or a way to fast-track budget approvals for time-sensitive experiments in paid media.

Some of these changes can be decided by the team alone. Others may require the approval of the marketing owner. And some may require buy-in from people outside the team, if they will affect other teams or stakeholders or entail allocation of additional resources. In these cases, the marketing owner or manager serves as a champion, advocating on the team's behalf to others in the company.

The goal is to encourage the team to think creatively about improving how it operates, intentionally countering the natural resistance to change. "That's the way we've always done it" shouldn't be a sufficient reason not to try something different. But the emphasis should be on *try*. Most changes should be approached as experiments that will be reviewed in later retrospectives. Did it make things better? Should we keep doing it or try something else?

We want to employ the same incremental and iterative thinking to our processes that we do to our productions. This lets our marketing organization evolve in an agile way too.

No Rules, except Your Own

By now, you should have a pretty good feel for the basics of agile management, primarily drawn from the Scrum methodology. There are plenty of great books, websites, training courses, and blogs from which you can learn more[1] and many variations of agile and lean practices that you can study. But hopefully this has given you a solid foundation.

More than anything, I'd encourage you to think of the agile marketing practices described here as a starting point. If this approach works for you as is, that's great. But if you like some aspects, but not others, that's okay too. Feel free to invent your own variation that is tailored to your needs.

Better yet, let your team develop its own variation through experience. That's what retrospectives every sprint cycle are intended to facilitate.

Of course, that's not to say that you shouldn't define and clearly state your own agile marketing process, even if it's a continuously evolving one. You want everyone on the team to understand it and buy into it, because the spirit of agile blossoms through transparency and ownership.

There is no universally right or wrong formula for agile marketing. All that matters is what is right for you. Really, the only wrong choice is to be unwilling to try new approaches in a world that is changing so rapidly around you.

There are no rules, except the ones you create.

Bring the hacker way to *how* you work.

Innovation

18

Moving Marketing from Communications to Experiences

Agility is an enabler. It gives us the ability to maneuver in a world of fast-moving digital dynamics. But our purpose for that agility is often to achieve greater *innovation*. We don't want to simply accelerate our reactions to competitors. We want to take the lead.

Marketing has always had a close relationship with innovation. Innovation in products and services has historically provided the best material for us to promote and differentiate our firm. "New and improved!" But marketing was usually more about creatively communicating our company's innovations, rather than innovating the nature of marketing itself.

The digital world has changed that, with an explosion of new marketing-led touchpoints with prospects and customers. The form that marketing takes, the way that we deliver it, and the overall experience that our audience has with it are all elements by which we can innovate new *ways* of marketing, not just new messages.

The most significant change that has unlocked opportunities for marketing innovation is this: Marketing has expanded from the design and delivery of *communications* to the design and delivery of *experiences*.

What we tell prospects and customers is still important. But how they experience touchpoints with our company has become even more important.

How does your website work when someone visits it? What if he or she visits it on a mobile phone? What helpful services, not just information, do you offer prospects who connect with you on the Web? How does your company react when people engage with you in social media? How relevant are the e-mails that you send when nurturing prospects? What calls to action do you offer them? How targeted and personalized are advertisements that you match to them as they move along a buyer's journey with you? How well synchronized are interactions on the phone or in person?

The ways in which these touchpoints work—and the degree of delight they deliver when people interact with them—actively shape perceptions of your brand. Directly, in the minds of those who engage with you. And indirectly, through what those people then say about you in social media.

Experience is the battlefield of modern marketing.

And it is rich with opportunities for innovating the practice of marketing itself.

Messages, Media, and Mechanisms

More than 50 years ago, Marshall McLuhan famously coined the phrase "The medium is the message."[1] Much of the innovation in marketing over the past five decades can be attributed to the creative interplay between messages—what is communicated—and media—how and where it is communicated.

McLuhan's insight was that the medium through which a message is delivered becomes an integral part of the message itself in the mind of the recipient. Taking out a full-page letter in the *New York Times* communicates something different than running a daytime television ad—even if the words written in the letter and spoken in the ad script are exactly the same.

Different media provide us different palettes for crafting the art of our messages. Spoken media has dimensions of tone, timbre, and the sequence and pacing of what is said within a window of time. Visual media has dimensions of shape and color. Video combines these, with a powerful ability to bring imagery, motion, and sound together. Physical media affects its messages by location and, in some instances, three-dimensional form.

Digital media brought new aspects to the expression of messages. The most fundamental breakthrough was hyperlinking—the links between different Web pages—which gave marketers a new dimension by which to craft messages: *the way they are interconnected.*

The digital dynamic of adjacency is an outgrowth of this, which has sprouted professional specialties from search engine optimization (SEO) to information architecture in website design. Adaptability—the ability to change digital media easily and personalize it at near zero cost—has altered how we create and deliver messages too, making them more fluid and customizable at scale.

We're still discovering the innovative possibilities that adjacency and adaptability offer us. But there's an even more powerful axis for innovation in a world of marketing experiences: how those experiences work.

In addition to messages and media, experiences can also have *mechanisms*, as illustrated in Figure 18.1.

Messages are what is communicated. Media is how and where it is communicated. And, in an experience that offers functionality and interactivity, mechanisms are *what the experience does* and *how it behaves.*

Mechanisms are more than the underlying functional capabilities of the medium itself. For instance, although the Web technically lets users click, scroll, zoom, and type or speak input,

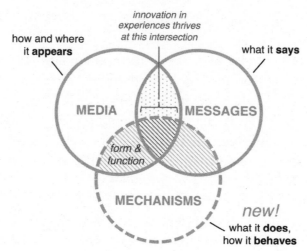

FIGURE 18.1 Marketing Is Realized through Messages, Media, and Mechanisms

those capabilities become interesting only when they are interwoven into an experience.

When those raw interactive elements are combined into a service—from something as simple as a sign-up process for a newsletter subscription to an advanced configurator that lets visitors build and order their own customized versions of your product—they acquire meaning to your audience. The designer of that service is able to shape the experience that the user will have and the meaning that he or she will infer from it.

Those meaningful interactions are mechanisms.

Just as messages become entangled in the media through which they're delivered, mechanisms become an integral part of communicating ideas and ideals to your audience. If your newsletter subscription service asks too many sales qualification questions, subscribers may assume your newsletter is more promotional than educational. If your product configurator is hard to use, prospects may conclude that your actual product is difficult to use too.

The mechanisms built into the experiences you deliver to your audience communicate characteristics about your company, as much as any words or images. Possibly even more, because what you do—the action in an experience—often carries more weight than what you say.

For experiences, *the mechanism is the message.*

This is both a cautionary warning and an opportunity. It's a warning: If the experiences that prospects and customers have with any of your touchpoints are not good, it will reflect poorly on your brand. And whether you have thought them through carefully or not, you inherently have mechanisms in almost all of your touchpoints. They either work well or don't work well, from a website, to a mobile app, to an automated call center. If those mechanisms fail to live up to your audience's expectations, they sabotage your marketing efforts.

Yet such mechanisms are also an incredible opportunity. They exponentially expand the number of creative options that you have to connect and engage with your audience. What services can you offer prospects along their journey that will catch their attention, help them achieve their goals, and—in the process—communicate the values of your brand? How can you improve the form *and* the function of the touchpoints they have with you to enchant and impress them?

Interactive Content

To get a better sense of the concept of marketing-led experiences as something different from classic marketing communications, let's look at the emerging field of *interactive content*.

Content marketing has grown in popularity over the past several years, especially as an alternative to traditional advertising. According to the Content Marketing Institute, "Content marketing is a strategic marketing approach focused on creating and distributing valuable, relevant, and consistent content to attract and retain a clearly defined audience—and, ultimately, to drive profitable customer action."[2]

However, to date, most of the content in content marketing has been *passive* in nature: blog posts, reports, e-books, white papers, webinars, podcasts, and so on. The audience reads, watches, or listens passively. The inspiration for this style of content marketing is often drawn from the entertainment industry and journalism. This is the brands-as-publishers meme.

Interactive content, contrasted in Figure 18.2, is *participatory* in nature: quizzes, games, calculators, assessment tools, configurators, solution finders, workbooks, and so on. The audience must actively *do things* with interactive content to experience it.

Mechanisms are the things they can do.

Interactive content goes beyond delivering information to an audience to providing useful *services*: a calculator to figure out cost of ownership, an assessment to see how your household or company compares against benchmarks or best practices, a configurator to compare different combinations of product options, a quiz to discover what you know—or don't know—about a relevant subject, and other handy utilities.

Research has shown that interactive content is more effective than passive content at differentiating a company's marketing, educating prospects, and converting them into leads and

	Passive Content	Interactive Content
Audience:	Consumes	Participates
Delivers:	Information	Services
Innovation:	Media	Mechanisms
Examples:	Blogs	Assessments
	E-Books	Calculators
	Infographics	Configurators
	Reports	Games
	Webinars	Quizzes
	White papers	Workbooks
Analogous Fields:	Entertainment, Journalism	Software Development, Consulting, Education

FIGURE 18.2 Comparing Passive Content and Interactive Content

customers. It's also more likely to be shared by prospects through social media.[3]

Why? When done well, interactive content is more interesting. It pulls participants into a more immersive kind of storytelling around a brand. The functionality and flow of mechanisms let marketers paint a more vivid and unique picture of their company's character and value. And because interactive content is able to react to the input of each individual participant, it's able to be more valuable and relevant to them—the key properties of content marketing as defined by the Content Marketing Institute. It immediately responds to the choices and data they provide.

Interactive content draws inspiration from disciplines such as consulting and education more than publishing. How do you engage prospects in exercises that will teach them something new? How do you empower them with tools that will assist them in their buyer's journey?

But most of all, interactive content draws inspiration from software development. All the examples of interactive content we've discussed are, essentially, little software programs.

Marketing as User Experience

As marketing moves beyond communications, toward crafting experiences in the digital world, it increasingly overlaps with the discipline of software development. The creation of great experiences on the Web, on mobile devices, and at other digitally powered touchpoints is, for all practical purposes, equivalent to the art and science of great software design.

We can actually map the model of media, messages, and mechanisms in marketing to the user interface (UI), data, and code in software. Messages are data, the medium is the UI, and mechanisms are implemented through code.

The intersection of code, data, and UI is where the collective user experience (UX) of software is forged. Analogously, the intersection of messages, mechanisms, and media in marketing defines customer experience (CX) in the buyer's journey. Figure 18.3 compares marketing CX and software UX as mirror images of each other.

Because so many experiences in the digital world are rendered directly by software, these two models are effectively blending. Which means marketing can look to methods of innovation in software development to inspire new ways of connecting with its audience.

Of course, this doesn't mean that marketers need to become software engineers. A lot of digital customer experiences can be designed and implemented using software tools that don't require the marketer to do any coding—at least not in the way a computer programmer would write code. But logic, flow, input and output, data processing, and other programmatic ideas—as well as the concept of the UI and the overall UX—are applied by marketers to craft these experiences, from interactive content to marketing automation.

In the digital world, marketing *is* UX—and vice versa.

Given this union of software and marketing in digital experiences, Bob Lord, the global chief executive officer (CEO) of the

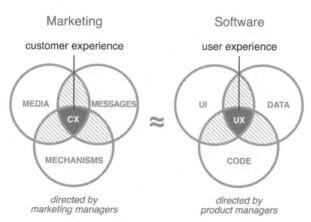

FIGURE 18.3 Parallels between Customer Experience (CX) and User Experience (UX)

digital agency Razorfish, and Ray Velez, the global chief technology officer of Razorfish, have suggested that modern marketers would be better off thinking about their roles as "product managers" more than marketing managers.[4]

Each of the touchpoints that marketing is responsible for can be thought of as a miniature product. A marketer takes ownership for that touchpoint. He or she focuses on understanding what the users—prospects and customers—really want from that touchpoint and creating the best possible UX for them that meets their needs. What do they want to accomplish? In what context? What are the barriers to their success, and how can they be overcome?

Like any other product manager, the owner of this marketing touchpoint pays attention to trends in the market that affect users' expectations. How good is this experience compared with the competition—or compared with best-in-class experiences from companies in unrelated market categories? How could the experience be upgraded with new features or a better UI? What new ideas can we test to learn more about our users and how to delight them?

By looking at touchpoints with our audience as product experiences more than merely marketing communications, we have a much bigger and more customer-centric canvas on which to innovate.

19

Marketing in *Perpetual Beta* with an Innovation Pipeline

Andrew Chen, one of the world's foremost growth hackers, cleverly coined "The Law of [Crappy] Clickthroughs" several years ago, which states: "Over time, all marketing strategies result in [crappy] clickthrough rates."[1]

Actually, Andrew used a harsher adjective than *crappy*, but this is a family book.

Having worked in product marketing for many years—after starting out as a software engineer early in his career, interestingly enough—Chen recognized a recurring pattern in digital marketing. As new marketing channels, strategies, and tactics were invented, they would generally perform well at first, but then their effectiveness would eventually degrade.

In his post defining this law, he gave a couple of examples. Display advertising on the Web started out with terrific clickthrough rates, which plummeted over time. E-mail marketing had excellent open rates—the percentage of recipients who read a message—at first, but then they declined too. This didn't apply just to clickthroughs but also to the efficacy of any marketing program.

Why? He described several reasons. First, the novelty of a new kind of marketing catches an audience's attention initially, giving it a performance boost, but that novelty eventually wears off. Second, if pioneering marketers are having success with something, other marketers are sure to follow, ramping up competitive noise. And third, as marketing ideas that worked with a small, initial audience are scaled up, they often end up reaching less qualified prospects.

All of these factors conspire to make success with any one particular marketing strategy or tactic temporary. And the digital dynamics of speed, scale, and adjacency serve to accelerate their rate of decline. The half-life of successful marketing tactics is shrinking.

The only answer to this Sisyphean challenge is to *continually innovate* your marketing, as illustrated in Figure 19.1.

Marketing must accelerate the rate at which it discovers and exploits new strategies, new tactics, and—in a digital world that is still creating them—even new channels.

The previous section on agility described *agile marketing*, a management methodology for operating at the tempo required to achieve this. But iterative and incremental implementation of ideas, informed by short feedback loops, is only as effective as the ideas that are prioritized in your backlog.

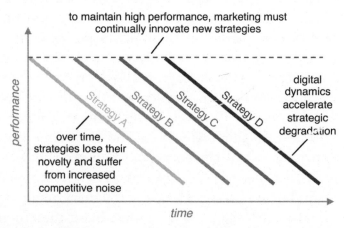

FIGURE 19.1   The Recurring Challenge of Andrew Chen's "Law of [Crappy] Clickthroughs"

Agile marketing gives managers and marketing owners a way to mitigate risk, by quickly trying out small versions of ideas to gauge their potential. But it relies on managers to encourage and nurture new ideas—and to be willing to allocate time and money to take those risks.

If your company culture is risk averse—*fail never* instead of *fail fast*—that can be a difficult shift in thinking to embrace. But to escape the downward gravitational pull of Chen's "Law of [Crappy] Clickthroughs," risks must be taken. In a digital world, the status quo is unstable.

Echoing "The Hacker Way": "The riskiest thing is to take no risks."

Minimum Viable Promotion

As suggested in the previous chapter, let's trade the hat of a marketing manager for that of a product manager for our prospect and customer touchpoints. Given the parallels between marketing and software that we've seen, what ideas for fostering innovation can we borrow and adapt from software product managers?

Arguably the most important concept in software product management today is the notion of a minimum viable product (MVP). Popularized by Eric Ries in his book *The Lean Startup*, an MVP is the smallest or simplest incarnation of a product that a company believes will resonate with its target audience. It's usually intended to prove—or disprove—a hypothesis about the market. "Would people like, use, or buy something like this?"

By "minimum," the intent is to invest the least amount of time, money, and effort necessary to try something before we know whether the product idea will even be appealing to people. But the MVP also has to meet the criterion of being viable. It can't be so stripped down that it fails to deliver something genuinely valuable or interesting. It certainly can't give people a bad or broken experience.

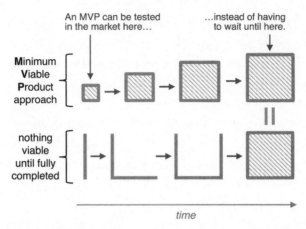

FIGURE 19.2 Conceptual View of an MVP Approach to Building Products (and Marketing)

Figure 19.2 illustrates a conceptual view of building an MVP.

Finding the right balance between *minimum* and *viable* can be hard. It forces product managers to really focus on the essence of their idea, making sure they clearly understand what the core benefit of the product will be to a particular audience. Referring to Clay Christensen's milkshake marketing, the product manager should be able to crisply answer the question "What job would different kinds of customers hire this product to do?"

Clarity about what constitutes *minimum viable* is crucial for developing an MVP. But it also serves to sharpen the team's vision of what it's building, for whom, and why.

If the results of the initial MVP are promising, then the team can iteratively improve it. If the MVP doesn't catch on, the team can try other variations to hone its hypothesis or— in the language of *The Lean Startup*—"pivot" to a different idea instead. The key advantage of MVPs is that they enable more ideas and variations to be tried, more quickly, with limited resources. An idea that doesn't work can afford to be rejected, or at least not allocated further investment.

You don't bet the farm until you test the water, if you'll forgive the mixed metaphor. That is why the concept of the MVP is considered lean. You minimize the investment in ideas that haven't yet demonstrated viability in the market, thereby reducing waste.

MVPs aren't just for products. You can have an MVP of a service as well. The definition of *product* can be interpreted very broadly. In fact, software product managers often apply an MVP approach to individual features that are being proposed as extensions or improvements to an existing product.

We can absolutely apply MVP thinking to marketing too.

When creating or changing marketing strategies, touchpoints, tactics, or campaigns, it can help to consider what an MVP version of that idea would look like. And if practical, test it in the real world before scaling it up.

It's stretching the definition of *product* a bit, so we can frame it as a *minimum viable promotion*,[2] in situations where that makes more sense. Any marketing touchpoint—a landing page, an e-mail, a search ad, a blog post, and so on—can be constructed as an MVP marketing experiment. But to make it meaningful, you should be able to answer these four questions:

1. What marketing hypothesis does this MVP test?
2. What metric(s) will serve as evidence of its success?
3. What value does this MVP offer its audience?
4. Does the quality of the MVP reflect our brand?

While the first two questions—a well-defined hypothesis and a concrete way to measure success—are central to minimum viable products and promotions, in software and marketing alike, the last two questions serve as a safety check to make sure that the experience prospects and customers have is positive.

An MVP could theoretically achieve a marketing objective—such as a certain number of leads or sales—but not necessarily result in customer happiness. By explicitly questioning the value that will be imparted to the people who engage with the MVP, we avoid inadvertently sacrificing customer goodwill in the blind pursuit of a metric. And questioning its quality helps ensure that our minimum still represents our brand in a positive light. Even if the MVP doesn't succeed by our internal yardstick, our audience should still have a good experience.

Prototypes and Perpetual Betas

Releasing an MVP out into the world is an important moment in the life cycle of a product or product feature—or equivalently, in a marketing strategy, tactic, or touchpoint. But what are the other stages before and after that moment?

Figure 19.3 illustrates where MVPs sit in a larger marketing innovation pipeline.

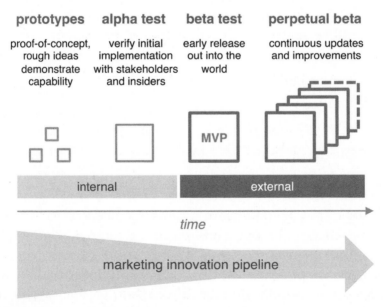

FIGURE 19.3 A Marketing Innovation Pipeline

In software, the earliest stage of development is usually *prototypes*: quick, little proofs of concept that demonstrate the feasibility of a new concept or a specific piece of a potential product. They're used inside the organization to confirm that something is possible and to solicit early feedback from peers and stakeholders. To quote Mark Zuckerberg from "The Hacker Way," "Instead of debating for days whether a new idea is possible or what the best way to build something is, hackers would rather just prototype something and see what works."

In user experience (UX) design, prototypes are often visual mock-ups, wireframes, and flow diagrams. They may be clickable, if they were built using a software tool. Or they may be simple *paper prototypes* that are printed out and posted up on a wall. The idea is to be able to rapidly share design ideas, which are easy to change, and stir productive discussion around them.

Most marketers have some experience with visual prototypes, such as when working on their website's design. Storyboards for videos, variations of a new brand identity, mock-ups of ads, early drafts of content, and models for trade show booths are all essentially prototypes too.

The beauty of a digital world is that almost *any* marketing touchpoint can be prototyped now, either as a visualization or as a demo of some new functionality in a software application.

Prototypes are generally low cost because not much time is invested in them. They are either implemented as rough ideas or kept to a very limited scope—or both. They are also low risk, other than the little bit of time spent on them, because they're not intended to be released to the outside world. These factors combine to make prototypes powerful vehicles for creativity.

One of the ways to grow marketing innovation is to *build more prototypes*, for more and different kinds of touchpoints. It's a great way to explore new possibilities and alternatives more frequently, inspiring more experimentation and learning. Even strategies and programs can be prototyped to a certain degree, with short slide decks that outline the thinking behind them, present relevant data, and display examples of what it might look like in practice.

When a prototype is a clear winner, that's wonderful—it can move on to the next stage. But not every prototype will move forward. The expectation should be that many won't, at least not in the way they're initially conceived. Some will be written off. Others will be worth keeping in mind for future opportunities. And still others will trigger ideas for different prototypes. All of this creative ferment is good though, because it helps free marketing from inertia.

Ideas that move forward from prototypes, to be built and deployed in the real world, often benefit from an *alpha test* stage. In software, an alpha test is typically an opportunity for people inside the company, or very close associates, to try the product before it's released to a broader audience. It's a chance to catch problems, known as *bugs*, and apply a little more polish.

In marketing, the nearest equivalent to alpha testing has been proofing—checking to make sure something looks correct before its release. However, the metaphor of alpha testing may be useful to encourage a wider review of new or updated marketing touchpoints, with fresh eyes and a greater emphasis on the flow of the overall experience. It's more than just proofing the content.

The next stage in software is a *beta test*, when the product is initially released out into the world—although possibly to a limited audience—but with the caveats that there may be a few bugs and that the product will likely undergo changes. The beta test is the first opportunity for a minimum viable product to really test its hypothesis in the market. Beta tests are usually closely monitored, to study how people react to the product and to fix any unexpected issues that arise.

Marketing has done things similar to beta testing, such as trying a new campaign in a test market first or running a pilot program. But traditionally, much of what marketing produced was released immediately into the world and presumed complete upon its distribution. It wasn't framed as a test. It was considered finished, and the team would move on to its next task.

Adopting agile marketing practices—more iterative and incremental approaches that leverage feedback from the real world—helps shift that worldview. Treating more tactics and touchpoints as MVPs, with their initial release as a beta test, puts us in a mind-set where we are expressly testing hypotheses about the market more regularly. This keeps the wheels of innovation in motion.

Before the Internet became the primary channel for software delivery, software products generally went directly from beta test to final release. With final release, the product, or at least that version, was considered done.

But in today's always-connected digital environment, where updates to software can be immediately pushed live to a website or a mobile app, the line between beta testing and final release has blurred. Software developers can deliver more incremental versions, more frequently, so that the product continuously evolves in the market. At any given time, some new feature of the product might be in beta test, even while the rest of the product is effectively as stable as a final release.

This mode of continuously testing new features is sometimes known as *perpetual beta*.

Marketing is undergoing a similar transition, thanks to the digital dynamics of speed and adaptability. Instead of episodic campaigns that are defined by their final release of a creative, campaigns can rapidly evolve with a series of creatives that are adjusted based on feedback from earlier versions. Many marketing touchpoints—such as websites, social media, e-mail marketing programs, and marketing automation—are now *always on* and can be updated any time.

So, could we approach marketing touchpoints as being in perpetual beta too?

It's certainly technically feasible to do so, and it mostly requires only a shift in the way we think about these touchpoints.

Instead of viewing them as done at any given point, we view them as continuously evolving works in progress.

That doesn't mean we're changing *everything* all the time or that all our changes have to be large in scope. But it does mean that anything in our marketing universe is a *candidate* to be changed at any time—even with just small, incremental changes that are slipstreamed into production.

In a perpetual beta, we regularly revisit all of our touchpoints, watchful for signs of decay or disruption, and favor a willingness to test new ideas and retest old assumptions. Any touchpoint that has gone too long without change—or at least an explicit confirmation that it's still meeting our expectations and is a good user experience—should be flagged for attention.

We favor a willingness to change to keep ahead of "The Law of [Crappy] Clickthroughs."

And it's not a big deal because, hey, we're in beta. Things are *meant* to change.

All four of these stages of marketing development, from prototypes to perpetual betas, can be viewed collectively as a pipeline for continuous marketing innovation. By keeping the pipeline filled with initiatives at each stage, a marketing team can nurture a steadier flow of new ideas to stay ahead of both competition and entropy.

20

Collaborative Designs and the Quest for New Ideas

Everybody innovates.

That's the philosophy many modern software development teams embrace. Rather than isolate responsibility for innovation in a specialized group, every developer is encouraged to contribute fresh ideas to the team and to pursue, within reason, intriguing new possibilities as an integral part of accomplishing his or her work. This plants more seeds of discovery, and it makes people's jobs more interesting and fulfilling.

Marketing can benefit from this democratized model of innovation as well.

Although in larger companies it may make sense to have dedicated individuals or teams who are focused on particular emerging businesses and touchpoints—through an innovation center or a marketing lab—any company can construct a much broader innovation group by allocating time and money for exploratory activities across *existing* marketing teams.

Committing that time and money across a team can be a hard choice but a valuable one.

Time, Money, and Innovation

Because modern marketing has become so operationally intense—there is always more to do than hours in the day—it's
tempting to manage our teams at close to 100 percent capacity
with the work of the status quo. We can easily end up with little
or no slack in our schedules.

Many people have tried to run software teams that way
too. It's appealing to squeeze out as much heads-down work
as possible for short-term gains without wasting time, so to
speak, on things that have a less certain longer-term payoff.
That can be practical in short bursts, when it's truly crunch
time. But when it becomes a constant way of life, it leads to
serious problems.

One obvious problem is burnout. People get worn down
from stress and monotony.

But the more strategic problem is it assumes that the status
quo will continue. It assumes that the performance we're seeing from today's marketing tactics can be extrapolated into the
future. So why change? But recalling Andrew Chen's "Law of

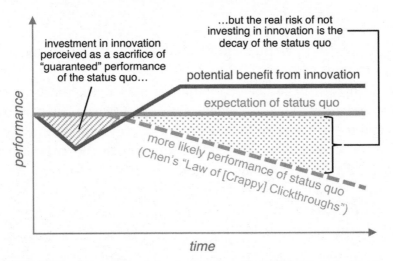

FIGURE 20.1   The Risk of the Status Quo Should Be Factored into
Marketing Innovation Investments

[Crappy] Clickthroughs" from the last chapter,[1] the more likely scenario is that the status quo will decay.

Clay Christensen, whom I previously introduced with milk-shake marketing, cowrote an article in *Harvard Business Review* that identified this assumption of the status quo as one of the biggest "innovation killers" in the corporate world. When managers calculate a discounted cash flow (DCF) or net present value (NPV) to decide whether a proposed new investment is worth it, they mistakenly compare it against existing cash streams. This presumes those cash streams will continue as is indefinitely. Instead, they should weigh new investments against the more likely probability that existing cash streams will likely erode if the company fails to pursue change.[2]

Both of these problems can be avoided by building into marketing schedules a little bit of time and money for innovation and spreading that across many of marketing's activities.

How much time and money? It depends.

Larry Page and Sergey Brin, the cofounders of Google, wrote in their company's initial public offering letter, "We encourage our employees, in addition to their regular projects, to spend 20 percent of their time working on what they think will most benefit Google. This empowers them to be more creative and innovative. Many of our significant advances have happened in this manner."[3]

At Facebook, according to "The Hacker Way," employees regularly set aside time for hackathons: "Every few months we have a hackathon, where everyone builds prototypes for new ideas they have. At the end, the whole team gets together and looks at everything that has been built. Many of our most successful products came out of hackathons."

Note that both Google and Facebook emphasize such exploratory innovation as a broad initiative. It's not limited to a specific lab or an innovation center.

For an example directly from marketing, consider the 70/20/10 model that Coca-Cola has used for allocating marketing budgets. In an *AdvertisingAge* article, its senior vice president of integrated marketing communications and capabilities, Wendy Clark, described how the company directs 70 percent of its budget to well-known programs—what we would call the status quo—20 percent to more innovative programs that have already shown some promise, and 10 percent to high-risk ideas that push into uncharted territory.[4]

The specific level of investment—20 percent of people's time or 10 percent of your budget—is not as important as the consistency of making regular and ongoing investments in innovation. Your company may choose to invest more or less, depending on your circumstances.

The important thing is to make some investment and to encourage everyone on your team to apply his or her intellect and imagination to invention and discovery. It's not just about *what* they work on but also equally about *how* they work on it that can be an opportunity to innovate.

Keep in mind the following quote, albeit slightly promotional, from Slack, a company that makes an app for team collaboration, about building in at least some "slack" into people's schedules: "Without slack, there is no reach, no play, no flexibility, no learning, no evolution, no growth."[5]

Collaborative Design for Marketing

Giving individuals on your marketing team the freedom and a mandate to explore new ideas on their own—enabled as a percentage of their time and budget—is one approach to fostering innovation across a wider team.

Another approach is to engage marketing teams in more collaborative design sessions.

In the field of user experience (UX) design, the *design studio* method has become popular for tapping a broader range of perspectives in the process of creating new products and features. It is a shift away from the classic division of responsibility, where a designer with a set of product requirements would go off to the mountaintop, summon inspiration, design the solution, and then bring back the answer for others to implement. In traditional advertising agencies, this was sometimes like the guru role of the creative director.

Instead, in a design studio, a cross-functional team comes together to cocreate a vision for how an experience should work. Although this method has been popularly applied in the context of building software and features on websites, it is actually a more general-purpose technique for collaborative design that we can apply to many kinds of marketing efforts.

A design studio, the general flow of which is illustrated in Figure 20.2, starts by assembling a diverse team of participants. In software projects, this typically includes a designer, a developer, a product manager, and other stakeholders. For a marketing project, this might be a group of several marketers but also people outside of marketing, possibly from sales, customer

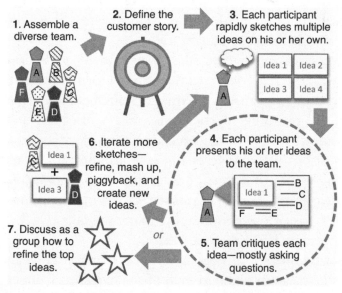

FIGURE 20.2 The General Flow of a Design Studio Exercise

service, or product development. The goal is to have a mix of perspectives in the room.

The person moderating the design studio kicks off the meeting by defining the problem that the team is going to solve or the customer experience that they're going to design. Ideally, it's a narrowly scoped mission. For instance, marketing might use a design studio to develop interactive content for the company's website, such as an assessment tool for prospects. The template of a customer story from agile marketing—describing *who* will use this and presumably *why*—is often a good place to start. Any additional context or constraints should be shared with the group as well. But *how* the problem will be solved, or the experience will be designed, is left wide open.

Next, each person takes 10–15 minutes to sketch several ideas on his or her own with pen and paper. You don't have to be good at drawing. The intent is to quickly generate as many concepts as possible, in a very rough form, of how this customer experience might be designed. The emphasis is on the *quantity* of ideas, not the quality of how they're represented. If you have five participants, and each of them outlines five ideas, that's $5 \times 5 = 25$ ideas! Even if many of them are similar, this process tends to explore a wide range of possibilities.

After that, each person takes a few minutes to describe his or her ideas to the rest of the team. It's not a formal presentation at all, just a quick explanation of the thinking behind each concept. In turn, all the other participants offer a brief critique—what they liked, what they were uncertain about, clarifying questions, or suggestions of possible changes. It's important to note that critiquing is *not* criticizing. "I don't like it" is not a helpful comment. Critiquing should be considered part of the brainstorming process, a positive way to imagine many possible tweaks to each design presented.

In a five-person group, if the other four participants each offers at least one critique to each of the five ideas from everyone else, that's now potentially $4 \times 5 \times 5 = 100$ variations examined.

Interesting suggestions and illuminating insights are annotated on worksheets or on a big whiteboard.

The next step of a design studio is to go back and do another round of individual sketches. Participants can refine or reconsider their own ideas based on the group's feedback. But they are also encouraged to piggyback on ideas from other teammates or to borrow pieces of them and create a mash-up of several concepts. This evolution on fast-forward, cross-pollinating parts of winning ideas with each other, while enabling new creative mutations. Ideas often combine in unexpected ways to produce a breakthrough.

Again, the group critiques all the ideas from that next round of sketches. At that point, the team can decide to either do another round of sketching, if there are still major new threads of possibility being uncovered, or move to a group discussion to refine the best ideas together.

Sketching and critiquing harnesses *divergent thinking*. Refining the best ideas together at the end harnesses *convergent thinking*. A healthy design studio session delivers the best of both worlds. It tends to produce good designs, strengthened by the diversity of thinking that went into them. At the same time, it engenders more shared understanding and connective thinking among the participants that has value beyond that specific design.

Design studios can be adapted to almost any marketing opportunity—website features, mobile experiences, social media response programs, prospect-nurturing campaigns, epic content marketing, and beyond. A team at my company recently used a design studio to rearrange the office layout to create a more productive and inspiring work environment.

Expand Your Palette of Inspiration

The seeds of innovation are ideas themselves. Although marketing has a terrific culture of creativity on its own, let's consider some of the techniques that software developers use to discover new ideas that we can borrow to expand marketing's innovation toolbox.

One method is to engage in the exercise of the 5 Whys. When dealing with something that didn't work as anticipated— in marketing's case, perhaps a campaign or touchpoint that failed to achieve its objectives—ask "Why?" But then ask "Why?" about that answer. And then "Why?" again, five times in total. This method, originally developed by Sakichi Toyoda, the founder of Toyota, is intended to push beyond surface-level symptoms to uncover deeper root causes.[6]

Here's a quick example of how the 5 Whys might work in a marketing context:

1. Why didn't our landing page convert more visitors? Because people didn't take our call-to-action offer.
2. Why wouldn't they have taken it? Either our offer wasn't attractive enough, or we were asking for too much with the call to action.
3. Why wouldn't the offer have been attractive if they intentionally clicked through to that landing page? Maybe where they clicked from led them to expect something else.
4. Why would they have expected something else? The ad or e-mail they clicked to get there may have had a mismatched message or, in context, implied something very different.
5. Why would that have happened? Our search advertising and e-mail marketing efforts are disconnected from landing page optimization on our website.

By the fifth *why*, we've gotten beyond just thinking about elements of the landing page—which is where most conversion optimization efforts are limited to and eventually peter out— into identifying a systemic disconnect between different marketing touchpoints that ultimately depend on continuity to succeed. We can now explore organizational or technological changes to rectify that problem. It becomes a much larger win than merely tweaking a landing page offer.

Engineers often try to turn lemons into lemonade. You may have heard a software person say, "It's not a bug, it's a feature!" And although that can sometimes be an excuse—if a customer is disappointed, it might as well be a bug—it does remind us that different people can approach the same touchpoint with very different expectations and intentions.

When that happens—on our website, in a marketing automation campaign, or through social media—instead of treating it as a problem that must be eliminated, it's worth considering how it may reveal a new opportunity. It may require different segmentation, or different choices for those particular prospects and customers, but is there a way to turn that into something good?

A quote that is often attributed to Isaac Asimov captures this potential beautifully: "The most exciting phrase to hear in science, the one that heralds new discoveries, is not 'Eureka!' but 'That's funny. . .'" When the unexpected occurs in your marketing, even if it's the result of an accident, take a moment to consider whether something new might have just been revealed.

Possibly the greatest source of inspiration, especially when thinking about what prospects and customers want through the lens of a product manager, is to *get out of the building.* That's the advice of Steve Blank, a successful Silicon Valley entrepreneur and renowned lecturer on entrepreneurship, who pioneered *customer development* as a parallel to traditional product development and whose ideas helped launch the lean start-up movement.[7]

Both marketers and software developers are prone to spending most of their time working in their own offices, where customers are abstracted into data and personas. Although that kind of inside work is necessary, Blank strongly encourages employees to literally get out of the building.

Go talk with customers and the kinds of people you hope to be your customers, face to face. Ideally, meet with them in their own environments, where you can directly observe how they deal with day-to-day situations. This kind of marketing anthropology reveals customer insights and associations that aren't visible through digital channels. It frequently triggers new ideas for how to better reach and serve your audience. And it cultivates deeper empathy with them.

And sometimes, simply a change of scenery can help stimulate fresh ways of looking at the world and the place your products and services have in it.

Take Blank's advice: Get out of the building.

There is a particular kind of customer who can be especially valuable to spend time with known as a *lead user*. The term was developed by Eric von Hippel, a professor of innovation at Massachusetts Institute of Technology (MIT) to describe customers who push the boundaries of existing products, often hacking them to do something beyond what they were originally designed for.[8] These customers are sometimes considered edge cases and outliers. But they can serve as leading indicators of where a market will be headed in the future or reveal the needs of new markets that aren't yet being addressed.

The shared theme across all of these approaches to seeking inspiration for innovation is to look outside your normal surroundings. Steve Johnson, author of the book *Where Good Ideas Come From: The Natural History of Innovation*, provides plenty of evidence that many of the greatest revolutionary ideas in history came from the "adjacent possible"[9]—opportunities that were simply one step removed from a common, accepted use case.

The more marketing explores beyond its everyday operations, the more innovations it will discover.

21

Big Testing Is More Important Than Big Data

Data has become the North Star of marketing and business. There's been an enthusiastic movement toward greater data-driven decision making in marketing, bringing more analytical rigor to a discipline that historically relied on gut instincts. There is still a vital role for instincts and intuition in marketing today, but data now provides more checks and balances on our gut, countering mental biases that can lead us astray.

The digital world has generated such an exponential explosion of data that the term *big data* emerged to describe this phenomenon. Big data has been described by its characteristics of volume, velocity, and variety. Volume is its enormous quantity. Velocity is its accelerated rate at which new data is generated and processed. And variety is its diverse range of different kinds of data, in structured and unstructured formats, all pooled together.

Big data has been widely heralded for its potential, in conjunction with machine learning technologies, to provide predictive analytics—answering, for instance, Which of your prospects have the highest propensity to buy and the largest likely lifetime values?—and better automated personalization for many customer touchpoints. These are very exciting developments.

193

However, big data is still largely a seed from which bigger things must be grown.

Data by itself is inert. It sits there until somebody, or some software program, does something with it. Data can inform the actions we take, but it is up to us to make it actionable.

One of the simplest yet most powerful ways we can activate data is through testing. We can find interesting patterns in our data, use them to form hypotheses, and then run experiments to determine whether those hypotheses can be effectively harnessed in our marketing. The results of those experiments are often the most valuable inputs into data-driven decision making.

Not all data is created equal. The quality of data can vary tremendously, from *dirty data* with inconsistencies and inaccuracies to *clean data* that has been scrubbed of such cruft. The meaning of a particular set of data can also depend heavily on its context—when and where it was collected, how, from whom, and what intentions they had—which isn't always in our line of sight. We have to be careful not to prematurely leap to conclusions.

In particular, exploring big data frequently uncovers interesting correlations, two or more things that appear to be related. But, as data scientists are quick to point out: Correlation is not necessarily causation.

To demonstrate that one thing actually *causes* another to happen requires an experiment. Ideally, we keep everything else constant and test the effects of changing only that one variable on our outcome, which is a *controlled experiment*. That's not always perfectly feasible, especially in marketing experiments over time, but we pragmatically do the best we can.

That is the heart of the scientific method.

The *science of marketing* involves more than simply left-brain analytical thinking, which is a popular interpretation of that phrase. To embrace science in our work, we must view nearly everything in marketing as a hypothesis to be tested and retested.

Luckily, testing in digital marketing is easier than in most other disciplines, thanks to the adaptability of digital. It's relatively straightforward to build most experiments using A/B testing features within many marketing software applications. Marketing typically has access to enough prospects or customers on which to run experiments to attain statistical significance for its test results. And most marketing experiments, when run carefully, are relatively low risk.

Therefore, although big data is important to modern marketing, a much bigger opportunity is *big testing*—an organizational capability to test and experiment continuously on a large scale.

What makes big testing *big*? Three principles:

1. A willingness to test *big ideas*.
2. A *big tent* that encourages widespread testing across the company.
3. An executive commitment to testing that makes it a *big deal*.

In turn, big testing gives us the ability to pursue bolder ideas responsibly in our business, by being able to prove them on a small scale before ramping them up. It gives us the confidence to create *big experiences*, the kind of remarkable customer experiences that stand out from the competition.

We can think of these as concentric circles, as shown in Figure 21.1, with big data at the core, surrounded by big testing to prove or disprove hypotheses about our market, which then enable big experiences for our audience. As we move outward, from internal analysis to affecting the external world, we increase the momentum of action fueled by data.

Let's dive deeper into each of the three principles of big testing.

What ultimately matters is creating remarkable customer experiences.

What makes big testing big?

1. Big Ideas
Meaningful learning is more important than minor optimization.

2. Big Tent
Many across the organization are empowered to run tests in their domain.

3. Big Deal
Executives vocally support a culture of experimentation.

Exploring big data helps us generate new hypotheses to test.

FIGURE 21.1   Big Data, Big Testing, and Big Experience

Big Testing Seeks Big Ideas

As we discussed in the previous chapter, the seeds of innovation are ideas themselves. The first principle of big testing is a willingness to seek out and try big ideas. An idea is *big* when it pushes the boundaries of the status quo, explores new ways to engage our audience, or seeks to validate a meaningful hypothesis about our business.

You might think of Steve Jobs as the patron saint of big ideas: "Think different."

We can contrast big ideas with the small ideas that are frequently tried when optimizing a digital marketing program, such as testing minor variations in presentation. For instance, trying different headlines or button colors on a landing page is usually small-idea optimization. Such optimization can still be quite valuable and help us maximize our outcomes. But to move the needle more significantly, we often need to experiment outside the existing structure. Instead of merely tweaking the presentation of a concept, we want to try *alternative concepts*, which might deliver new and different functionality and flow to the buyer's journey or offer fundamentally different propositions to the market.

For example, instead of just testing variations of a landing page that offers an e-book, we might test that concept against two very different alternatives: a landing page that promotes a webinar on the same material and an interactive assessment tool that lets participants evaluate their own readiness and suitability for a relevant solution.

After determining which of those concepts has the greatest impact, we can then follow up with subsequent optimization tweaks to refine the winner further.

One way to visualize the difference between big-idea experimentation and small-idea optimization is to picture an infinitely long chart that represents all the possible ideas that we could implement for a particular touchpoint with a prospect, as in Figure 21.2. For each idea, the chart shows how well it will perform. Ideas that are similar, with just small differences among

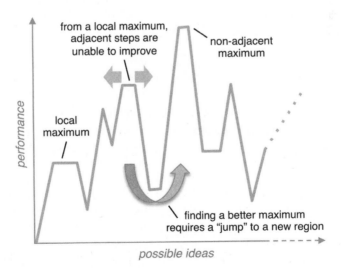

FIGURE 21.2   Innovation Requires Exploration Beyond a Local Maximum

them, are located close to each other. Ideas that are dissimilar are located farther away.

Small-idea optimization starts at a point in that chart and takes small steps—by making small changes—to see whether a higher-performing variation is nearby. However, after exploring that local region of the chart for a while, and finding the highest point it can, it usually hits a ceiling where it seems unable to do any better. That point is known as a *local maximum*. It's probably not the highest-performing point on the entire chart—in other words, not the *global maximum*. But it's the highest one we can reach by taking adjacent steps.

To do better, we need to jump to a different spot on the chart, farther away. That is the leap of a big-idea experiment. There's no guarantee that any one region we leap to will be better, but trying a number of far-reaching hops before settling into stepwise optimization improves the odds that we will discover fertile ground.

By the way, for a little piece of nerdy trivia, the connection between marketing and software here is that this approach—big leaps followed by small steps—mimics a very effective machine learning algorithm known as *simulated annealing* that estimates the optimal parameters of a function.

How do you know if an idea is *big* enough?

One gauge of a big idea is to ask this question: If the experiment succeeds or fails, what will I have learned about my audience in the process? If there's an opportunity for the outcome to teach us something meaningful about our market that we can leverage moving forward—"validated learning" in the language of *The Lean Startup*—that makes an idea big.

Coming up with big ideas can be hard work, but that's where competitive advantage can be discovered. Many of the brainstorming techniques covered in the previous chapter can help. For instance, design studios are often highly conducive to generating big ideas.

It's also worth reflecting for a moment that the difficulty of formulating good hypotheses and devising effective ways to test them is what makes science a *creative* discipline as much as an analytical one.

When we talk about the science of marketing, we're not exorcising creativity out of the profession. On the contrary, we're elevating it to a guiding operational principle.

Big Testing Opens a Big Tent

The second principle of big testing is a *big tent*. Many people across the organization are empowered and encouraged to run experiments as a part of their work. Testing isn't restricted to a limited number of specialists. It's widely used for improving many aspects of the business.

There are three advantages to this more open approach to testing.

First, with the explosion of digital touchpoints, there are more opportunities to improve customer interactions than ever before. The sheer volume of Web pages, e-mails, ads, content, and social media is greater than any one testing czar or even a dedicated testing team could ever hope to conquer alone. Distributing testing capability across marketing helps us address a larger portion of these opportunities.

Second, nurturing widespread experimentation inoculates the organization from slipping into the inertia of the status quo. By continuously testing and retesting ideas and assumptions, the company is more likely to detect the early signals of shifts in its market. It will uncover new winning tactics more frequently because it actively seeks them out. Experimentation provides an engine for propelling continuous improvement.

And third, the act of designing and running tests helps people engage more deeply in their work. Running experiments inspires you to think about what you're doing in fresh ways. It opens a path for ongoing learning and development. And it is empowering to have the ability to try new ideas. Good testing is a skill and a mind-set that builds a valuable kind of organizational capital in the digital world.

For these reasons, big testing is a natural part of agile marketing. It is the meaning of the agile marketing value of *many small experiments over a few large bets.*

Of course, not all experiments are equal.

Depending on what kind of tests you're running, and where, you face different degrees of potential impact on your brand and more or less contention with other tests that may be running at the same time. For example, testing two versions of an e-mail for a content marketing offer targeted to a narrow audience segment probably has a limited scope in its potential brand impact. It's unlikely to interfere with other tests being run elsewhere in marketing at that time. On the other hand, a pricing test deployed on the home page of your website may have a significant impact on your brand, and any other experiments on pricing or run on the home page should be closely coordinated.

These scenarios are represented in the 2×2 matrix of brand impact versus test contention shown in Figure 21.3. Experiments

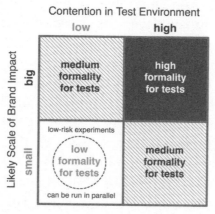

FIGURE 21.3 Different Levels of Formality for Different Kinds of Marketing Experiments

with small brand impact and low contention don't need much formality in how they are managed. Many of them can be run in parallel. Experiments with big brand impact and high contention, such as a pricing test on the home page, should have a high degree of formality in how they're governed. Experiments in the other two quadrants benefit from some oversight, but they shouldn't be bottlenecked by too much management overhead.

A testing czar or testing team can serve as the central authority for coordinating tests that need some level of formality to be implemented safely. But that role should be an enabler, more than a gate, to train and support broad testing efforts across the entire organization. The number of properly run tests executed throughout the company becomes a metric of its success.

Big Testing Is a Big Deal for Leadership

Finally, the third principle of big testing is that executives vocally support a culture of experimentation across the organization. They make a big deal of it. It's a top-down endorsement, even a mandate, for employees to embrace testing as an integral part of their jobs.

You know testing is a big deal at a firm when the chief executive officer emphasizes it in his or her annual letter to shareholders. For example, Jeff Bezos boasted that Amazon.com had run 1,976 experiments to improve its website and products in 2013—up from 1,092 such experiments in 2012 and 546 in 2011.[1] That's more than 80 percent growth in experimentation each year.

You know testing is a big deal at a firm when it becomes renowned for the large number of experiments it runs—and is proud even if only a small percentage of them prove fruitful. For instance, Jim Manzi reported in his book *Uncontrolled: The Surprising Payoff of Trial-and-Error in Business, Politics, and Society* that Google ran approximately 12,000 experiments in 2009, with only about 10 percent of them successfully leading to business change.[2] By being willing to try so many ideas, even if many of them didn't pan out, Google uncovered around 1,200 meaningful changes to improve its business.

Of course, Amazon.com and Google are both giant, digitally native companies, so the quantity of experiments that they run is naturally on the high end. But the underlying principle driving them applies to every business in a digital world.

One of the best ways that executives can communicate the importance of testing in their company's culture is to champion the agile marketing value of *testing and data over opinions and conventions.*

Everybody has opinions. Traditionally, and especially in marketing, it was typically the opinion of the boss that would determine the course of action to be taken. The popular analytics blogger Avinash Kaushik called this the HiPPO—the highest-paid person's opinion.[3]

With experimentation, opinions can transform into hypotheses. There can be several competing opinions, and the easiest solution to determine which one is the right choice is to run a test. This lets your prospects and customers pick the winner empirically. It's their opinion that ultimately matters most.

In a culture of big testing, executives don't treat their own opinions as exceptions to this test-driven approach. They gladly propose them as hypotheses to be tested. And if their idea doesn't win, they use it as a teaching moment to demonstrate why testing is better than unchecked intuition.

The same applies to conventions. Although it's important to respect traditions that are part and parcel of your brand, too much deference to "the way things have always been done here" can end up being an excuse for inertia. In a big-testing culture, executives permit careful testing of the company's conventions from time to time, to revalidate assumptions about the market. As the saying goes, sometimes sacred cows make the best hamburgers.

Big testing uses all of these principles to maximize the volume, variety, and velocity of experiments—analogous to the defining characteristics of big data. It becomes the machinery of innovation to validate new ideas.

And then we have to scale them.

IV

Scalability

22

Bimodal Marketing

Balancing Innovation and Scalability

As our marketing innovation gains momentum, we should take a moment to celebrate. It's a great feeling to be sailing into the future with the digital wind at your back.

But that moment is quickly followed by the realization of another challenge: *scalability*.

It's one thing for an idea to work on a small scale, where the person or people who invented it are able to nurture it carefully. They're immersed in the concept and understand how it works better than anyone. They can tinker with the concept, and they usually focus on feasibility—demonstrating that the idea can work—more than repeatability or consistency.

Scaling up those ideas—adopting them more widely or deploying them more frequently throughout marketing—is a different matter entirely. Sometimes scaling marketing is simply a matter of *reach*: distributing communications or experiences to a larger audience. But it can also require greater *participation* inside the company: more people who must understand the concept and the role they play in its execution. Repeatability and consistency become very important.

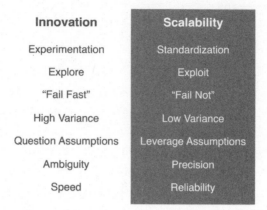

FIGURE 22.1 The Opposing Characteristics of Innovation and Scalability

Marketing faces an additional scalability challenge today, resulting from the enormous *variety* of touchpoints under marketing's umbrella. Instead of a small number of programs that are simply being scaled by growing their external reach and internal participation, marketing now manages an increasing diversity of programs overall, of many sizes and flavors. And, thanks to the ever-shifting world of digital dynamics, that portfolio of programs is continuously evolving.

These are not easy challenges to solve. However, they do echo many of the same hurdles of scalability that software development and information technology (IT) professionals wrestle with in their work. And again, we can borrow and adapt some of their frameworks and techniques for managing them.

To further appreciate these challenges, though, it's worth recognizing that the values and objectives of innovation and scalability are often diametrically opposed, as shown in Figure 22.1.

Innovation is about experimentation.
Scalability is about standardization.

Innovation explores many new possibilities.
Scalability exploits the promising ones.

Innovation encourages a "Fail fast" approach.
Scalability strives for "Fail not" robustness.

Innovation has high variance in its outcomes.
Scalability optimizes for low variance.

Innovation questions assumptions about the business.
Scalability leverages assumptions.

Innovation harnesses ambiguity.
Scalability harnesses precision.

Innovation values speed.
Scalability values reliability.

These are dichotomies, and when you compare their key characteristics side by side, you realize just how dissimilar they can be from one another. The tricky part is that every business—and every marketing department—needs a combination of both innovation and scalability, in some balance of the two. Yet there is an inherent tension between them.

What management approach could hope to serve both ends of this spectrum without, to some degree, either stifling innovation or compromising scalability?

The Edge and the Core

The answer is not one management approach but two.

Ideas that are being incubated as innovations are managed one way. Programs and capabilities that are being scaled up across marketing, or are viewed as a more fundamental part of the business, are managed a different way.

Essentially, we divide marketing into two realms, as shown in Figure 22.2: the *edge* of our organization, where innovations emerge, and the *core* of our business, where reliable operations run at scale.

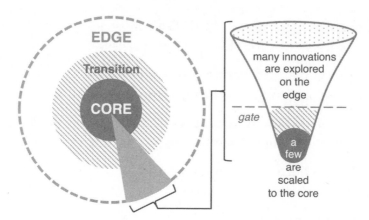

FIGURE 22.2 Managing Marketing in Two Realms: The Edge and the Core

As a mnemonic, think of the *leading edge* and *core competencies*, respectively.

Projects and campaigns on the edge are managed according to the values and objectives of innovation: Try new ideas, fast, and learn from them. The edge is the realm of prototypes and MVPs—minimum viable products and promotions. As long as the basic principles of the brand are respected, there's more leeway to bend the rules. Administrative overhead is kept to a minimum, with few formal processes or documentation requirements. After all, there's no point in institutionalizing these ideas until they're proven and ready to scale, because the far majority of them won't make that cut. New software tools and service providers can be fast-tracked into pilot programs, with some caveats around their scope and relatively lightweight integration.

In contrast, programs and capabilities at the core are managed according to the values and objectives of scalability: robust and reliable touchpoints for prospects and customers, repeatable campaign execution, and dependable marketing operations. Processes are generally well defined and documented. Rules and standards are more strictly enforced. Knowledge is institutionalized with more formal training and onboarding. Software tools and data are managed more centrally, with tighter controls and deeper integration. Vendors are more thoroughly vetted. A wider set of stakeholders are consulted when changes are made in this realm.

This dual approach is partially inspired by the concept of *bimodal IT*, also known as two-speed IT, advocated by the analyst firm Gartner. It defines *bimodal IT* as "The practice of managing two separate, coherent modes of IT delivery, one focused on stability and the other on agility. Mode 1 is traditional and sequential, emphasizing safety and accuracy. Mode 2 is exploratory and nonlinear, emphasizing agility and speed."[1] The key is that both of these modes operate simultaneously in the same company but work on different projects and programs.

In our language, we'd associate Mode 1 with the core and Mode 2 with the edge. We can analogously call this *bimodal marketing*. But there are some important distinctions with bimodal marketing.

First, both the edge and in the core can—and should—be managed using agile marketing methods. Agile management lets us efficiently allocate resources and quickly adapt to feedback, which are equally desirable in both realms.

Second, marketing in the core is definitely *not* slow or static. It is continuously evolving and being optimized, with new experiments being run regularly. The difference is that the range of experimentation in the core is narrower, with guardrails and safety nets. We rely more on the assumptions of previously validated learning. There's more structure, but its purpose is to promote efficiency, not hinder progress. Performance metrics are relatively well established, with agreed-upon methods of measurement and a history of benchmarks for us to compare new iterations against. It's a well-oiled machine.

And third, the edge and the core are not necessarily separate teams. Ideally, every team in marketing should have a mix of efforts they're pursuing in both realms. The ratio between them will vary from sprint to sprint, team to team, and company to company, but as a rule of thumb, target approximately 70 percent investment in the core and 30 percent on the edge. Note that there may be a larger *quantity* of ideas explored on the edge, because only the strongest and most sustainable ones graduate to the core, but the majority of investment goes toward scaling in the core.

Edge-to-Core Transitions

That notion of graduation leads to the other inspiration of this edge/core framework, the use of *stage gates*, also known as phase gates, in research and development (R&D) and new product development funnels.

The journey of bringing a new product to life is divided into stages, from early research and prototypes, to field tests and trials, and then ultimately full-scale production. At each stage, the product is reviewed to determine whether the results so far warrant it proceeding to the next stage—a gate it must pass through to receive further investment. This process is often visualized as a funnel, because it starts with a large number of ideas in the early stages and then winnows down to a few that make it all the way through.

Now, most marketing innovations don't need a heavy, multistep stage gate process. But in leveraging open experimentation on the edge as a proving ground, we do want an orderly way to promote the winners—the best ones that show promise to scale—into the core.

Because the edge and the core operate in very different ways, this transition requires a shift in thinking. Issues that would have been premature on the edge become critical for success in the core. Will existing processes or organizational structures need to change, and how? Will existing elements in the core be replaced or extended? What is the scope of the rollout—a few markets or globally? Is there a road map for implementing it incrementally, in phases? How will resources be allocated to it? What are the metrics by which it will be operationally managed? What training will be necessary, at launch, over time, and for onboarding new staff down the road?

The advantage of separating the edge and the core is that we have to address those meaty issues only when we're ready to commit to scaling an idea. The creative ferment on the edge gives us *options* and insight into those options. But we aren't obligated to exercise them.

In this way, the transition phase from the edge to the core is effectively a stage gate. Ideas from the edge can be formally evaluated to determine whether they should move forward to the core.

However, not every idea needs to move from the edge to the core, even if it's been successful there. Some may have worked well in the small cases where they were experimentally developed but be deemed unlikely to be as effective at scale or as a more standardized part of marketing—at least relative to other investment choices in the core. That shouldn't be treated as a failure, and indeed the idea may continue running in the edge for as long as it's beneficial. But because it's not part of the core, it can fade away at any point with minimal disruption.

Maturity Models

Inside the core, not all programs and capabilities are at the same level or scale. They've been adopted as part of the mainstream marketing engine for the company, but they can vary significantly in how many resources are allocated to them and how much sophistication and expertise the organization has developed around them.

Picture this as a graph with two dimensions, like Figure 22.3: On one axis is the *scale* of the program or capability—how much capital, human and financial, is invested in it. And on

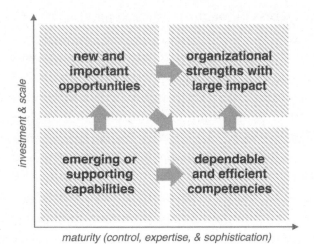

FIGURE 22.3 Capabilities in the Core Have Varying Levels of Scale and Maturity

the other axis is its *maturity*—how advanced the organization has become in operating it.

These two axes are often correlated, but not always. You might be really good at content marketing, a high level of maturity in how you execute and manage it, yet have limited budget allocated for it. Vice versa, you might invest a lot of money in producing and distributing content, because it's become a top priority, yet be early in the learning curve of figuring out how to run that program with the greatest effectiveness and efficiency.

Over time, programs and capabilities will likely shift quadrants, generally by maturing.

Although the axis of scale—the quantity of resources invested—is pretty straightforward to calculate and plan, the axis of maturity can be a little fuzzier. How should you measure maturity and plot its advancement?

One approach, which was pioneered in the software profession and has since migrated into marketing and many other disciplines, is the use of *maturity models*. Maturity models define a structured set of stages, or levels, that organizations typically progress through in developing a particular capability or competency.

One of the first maturity models was the Capability Maturity Model (CMM),[2] developed by the Software Engineering Institute at Carnegie Mellon University. Although its name sounds rather generic, it was originally intended to assess the ability of software developers contracted by the U.S. Department of Defense to produce promised deliverables.[3] Advancements in maturity were associated with greater predictability in a firm's software development processes. The model defined five levels, from an initial *ad hoc* condition ("Process? What process?") up to *optimizing*, where all processes are well defined, accurately measured, precisely controlled, and continuously improved.

Since it was introduced, the CMM has been adapted to many other process-oriented capabilities, mostly within the fields of IT and project management. But the concept of maturity models has grown even more broadly, from process predictability to more generally the notion of levels of sophistication and expertise within a particular discipline or competency.

In a typical five-level model, as shown in Figure 22.4, organizations are ranked as (1) novice, (2) practitioner, (3) intermediate, (4) advanced, or (5) expert, according to the goals and practices they've adopted. The fifth level is usually considered an ideal state to strive for, but one that is rarely attained.

The field of marketing has had an explosion of new maturity models proposed over the past several years, for specific disciplines such as Web analytics, content marketing, conversion optimization, search marketing, social media marketing, account-based marketing, and so on. If you search the Web for these, or for other kinds of marketing maturity models, you'll discover dozens of variations.

This naturally begs the question: Which are the *right* maturity models to use?

The answer is: It depends. Many models have been developed, by professional associations, analysts, consultants, and

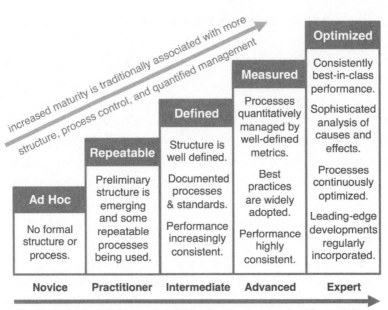

FIGURE 22.4 General Structure of a Five-Stage Maturity Model

marketing technology vendors. They all attempt to distill the best practices and recurring patterns that their creators have observed, across a wide range of organizations, into a logical progression of capabilities. Some are more biased than others, based on the commercial interests of the people who created them, and should be taken with a grain of salt. But even those models with their own agenda can be useful for learning what is possible.

You may want to draw upon several models to synthesize your own.

The power of maturity models is not that they're ironclad definitions of how a company must work but that they provide a framework by which an organization can systematically think through the rational evolution of its own capabilities. They offer a reasonable gauge for the maturity axis of competencies in our core. And they help manage expectations among stakeholders and inform management decisions about what degree of maturity a particular capability is worth.

That last point is important to recognize. A company shouldn't always pursue the highest level of maturity for every capability in its organization. After all, advancing the sophistication and expertise of any capability requires an investment of time, money, and mental energy. This often becomes exponentially more expensive with each additional level. We must prioritize those that are the most relevant to our strategy and competitive advantage.

Collectively, the strategic balance of innovation and scalability is determined by what we explore on the edge, what we bring into the core, and what level of scale and maturity we target for those core programs and capabilities.

23

Platform Thinking and Pace Layering for Marketing

Everything is connected.

That's probably true in a broad spiritual or metaphysical sense. But it's absolutely true in marketing—and in software architecture, for that matter. What a customer experiences at one marketing touchpoint influences his or her expectations and perception of your brand at subsequent touchpoints. Behind the scenes, processes and priorities in one area of marketing have ripple effects on other areas, whether it's a subtle and diffuse impact on the company's culture or a concrete trade-off in budget allocation.

The bonds between any two components of marketing may be strong or weak, direct or indirect. But changes in one will affect the other, in small or large ways, quickly or over time.

Although this has always been true, digital dynamics have multiplied and magnified these effects. The number of external touchpoints and internal moving parts in marketing's ecosystem has grown geometrically in recent years. Digital adjacency makes the bonds between previously dispersed pieces stronger and more direct. Digital speed and adaptability accelerate the rate of change. And digital scale amplifies their impact on the business.

If this sounds like it can easily become a tangled mess, you're right.

For example, a supposedly harmless upgrade to your website might contain a bug that inadvertently changes the Web locations, or uniform resource locators (URLs), of several key pieces of content. This might drop your ranking for certain keywords in Google's search listings, which in turn may increase the cost per click of your paid search ads. Links in your e-mail newsletter that went out the other day no longer work, so respondents who click get redirected to an unexpected Web page—and in the process a hidden campaign code is lost, so any actions those customers take aren't properly tracked in your marketing automation system, affecting subsequent steps in nurturing campaigns. Some confused customers might reach out to your social media accounts, which may not be able to replicate the problem because the website recognizes them as staff members and routes them in a different way to the original content. This compounds confusion in their responses. And so on.

You get the point. Modern marketing is a complex set of interdependencies that is subject to the *butterfly effect*—a small change in one area can result in big, unpredictable disruptions elsewhere.[1]

The frequency and effects of such unintended entanglement can be reduced or mitigated but not eliminated, as illustrated in Figure 23.1. After all, everything *is* connected. But one of our objectives in scalability, whether designing software or marketing, is to structure and arrange the different components of our solution so as to maximize synergy and minimize negative side effects.

In software, this structural arrangement of components is known as its *architecture*.

We'll examine several architectural concepts from the software world that we can adapt to the scalability of marketing, which are applicable to strategies, systems, processes, and even organizational structure. And we'll start by considering one of

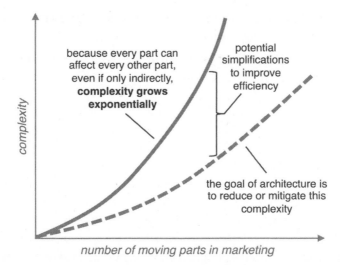

FIGURE 23.1   Exponential Complexity in Marketing, Tempered by Good Architecture

the most natural ways to differentiate the various components of marketing into groups logically: *the rate at which they change.*

Pace Layers for Marketing

Let's step back from marketing and software for a moment to examine something more tangible: buildings in the physical world. The architect Frank Duffy first argued that a building should not be conceived as a single object but rather as a collection of layers, and that each of those layers changes on a different time horizon. The author Stewart Brand expanded on this idea of *shearing layers* in his book *How Buildings Learn: What Happens After They're Built.*[2]

Brand defined six layers of buildings, from the slowest changing to the fastest:

1. The *site* on which the building has been constructed, which is essentially permanent

2. The core *structure* of the building, including its foundation and load-bearing elements
3. The outer *skin* of the building, such as its facade, external walls, and windows
4. The functional *services* in the building, such as plumbing and electrical systems
5. The *space plan* or layout, such as interior walls and doors that divide each floor
6. The *stuff* placed inside that layout, such as furniture, appliances, art, and so on

Because these layers naturally evolve at different rates, the key principle that Duffy and Brand advocated is to design buildings intentionally to facilitate such unsynchronized changes. For example, services infrastructure should be designed to enable easier reconfiguration of space plans. This architectural approach strives to make buildings more adaptable.

In a later book, *The Clock of the Long Now*, Brand offered an analogous pace-layering view of civilizations. He defined six pace layers in this context, from the slowest changing to the fastest: nature, culture, governance, infrastructure, commerce, and fashion.[3] Nature changes at a glacial pace, literally, while fashion is fleeting. It's a fascinating lens on the strata of change.

This framework of pace layering caught the attention of software and information technology (IT) professionals, as a useful model for designing systems with components that change and adapt at different rates. For example, Gartner created a Pace-Layered Application Strategy for "categorizing, selecting, managing and governing applications" according to their rate of change and their relative novelty—from common, stable *systems of record* to rapidly changing *systems of innovation*.[4] Gartner's model is actually relevant to marketers today for managing portfolios of marketing technology.

Jesse James Garrett adapted pace layers to user experience design in his book, *The Elements of User Experience: User-Centered Design for the Web*. He defined five *planes* of website experience, from the most abstract to the most concrete: strategy, scope, structure, skeleton, and surface.[5] For instance, information architecture is down at the *structure* plane, navigation and interface design, represented by low-fidelity wire frames, are part of the *skeleton*, and finally visual design, including color palettes and typography, represented by high-fidelity comps, are up on the *surface*.

Choices made on lower planes constrain the possibilities of what can be implemented in higher planes. Although there's less emphasis on each plane evolving on a different timescale, the architectural effect is the same: Higher planes can change independently from lower planes, within their established constraints, but the same is not true in the opposite direction.

Marketing overall can be viewed through the lens of pace layers too.

Picture seven layers on which marketing operates, as in Figure 23.2, from those that evolve most slowly to those that effectively change in real time.

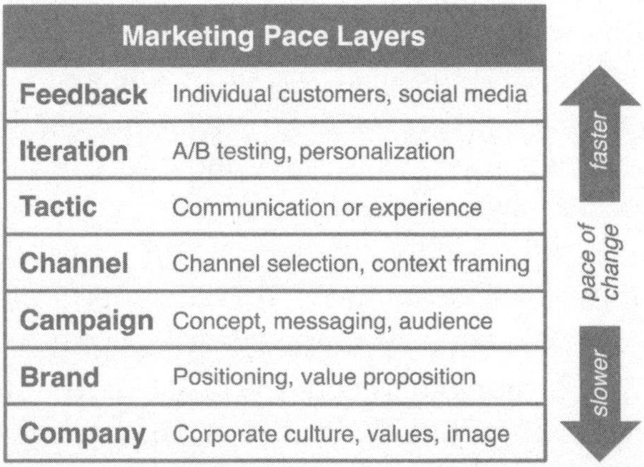

Marketing Pace Layers	
Feedback	Individual customers, social media
Iteration	A/B testing, personalization
Tactic	Communication or experience
Channel	Channel selection, context framing
Campaign	Concept, messaging, audience
Brand	Positioning, value proposition
Company	Corporate culture, values, image

pace of change: faster ↑ / slower ↓

FIGURE 23.2 The Seven Pace Layers of Modern Marketing

1. *Company.* The foundation of all marketing is a company's culture, its values, and its image, in the minds of both internal employees and the external market. Those characteristics of a firm are hard to change and move very slowly—a multiyear timescale. Corporate strategy at this level establishes the outer boundaries for the layers above.

2. *Brand.* The primary level for marketing strategy, brand is the layer that deals with the positioning and value proposition for a company's products and services, each of which may be its own brand, and developing a holistic understanding of target customers, the market, and the competitive landscape. This layer changes on a timescale of quarters and years.

3. *Campaign.* Campaigns are probably the sexiest layer of marketing, because they form the creative bridge between high-level strategy and tactical implementation of customer touchpoints. Both episodic campaigns and more continuous marketing programs are in this layer. Concepts—the big ideas—messaging, and audience segmentation are typically defined at this level. This layer typically operates on a timescale measured in months.

4. *Channel.* Campaigns are mapped into channels, and the decisions of which channels to select, for which times and with what allocation of investment, is a layer that can evolve independently within the structure of a campaign. This level is responsible for *context framing*—understanding how a campaign can best serve the needs of audiences, in the setting of each specific channel—and coordinating cross-channel synergies. Its timescale for change is weeks to months, because some aspects are closer to the slower campaign layer below, wheras others are closer to the faster tactic layer above.

5. *Tactic.* The design and development of specific communications or experiences within the framework of a brand, campaign, and channel happens at this layer. The pace of change here

runs from days to weeks, depending on the particular tactic. There can be a tremendous amount of creative liberty at this level and a lot of room for experimentation, if permitted.

6. *Iteration.* The deployment and distribution of communications and experiences can be categorized in its own level, especially with the speed and adaptability of digital environments. Iterations can A/B test alternative versions and use personalization logic to substitute content and services dynamically for different prospects and customers. Iterations being actively worked on may change on a timescale of days or possibly even hours in fast-moving social channels.

7. *Feedback.* Finally, thanks to social media, the signals of "digital body language" and explicit "digital dialogue" exchanges of data with prospects,[6] and closer alignment between sales and marketing, there's a superfast-moving layer of feedback from prospects and customers with which marketers can engage. It's possible to react to these interactions on a timescale of hours or minutes—or possibly even in fractions of a second with the help of computer algorithms.

This pace-layered model of marketing is certainly idealized. There's plenty of sloshing between layers in the real world, and their structure and timescales may differ in your company. But it helps us recognize some of the challenges that arise from these interlocking cogs moving at different speeds. Faster layers unintentionally constrained by slower ones. Confusion around which layer should adapt to a particular threat or opportunity. Tectonic shifts in the lower layers that cause unexpected earthquakes for people working above.

Similar to how other disciplines have approached pace layers, we can intentionally design marketing's *architecture* to take advantage of these layers, alleviate some of those cross-layer challenges, and better support the right kind of adaptation at each level.

Layers, Partitions, and Platforms

In general terms, there are two architectural strategies that software developers employ to achieve scale that we can borrow as a broader metaphor: *layers* and *partitions*, as illustrated in Figure 23.3.

Layers, such as pace layers, are conceptually stacked on top of each other and are usually illustrated as horizontal slices. Things higher up in that layered stack depend on and regularly communicate with what's below them. Partitions, on the other hand, are a way of dividing things into separate groups that operate more independently of each other. Changes in one partition typically do not affect the other partitions. They're often illustrated as vertical slices.

Most software programs of any real significance have a mix of both layers and partitions.

Organizational structures apply these same concepts too. We can think of shared services, support capabilities, and

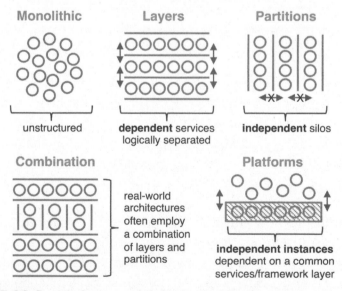

FIGURE 23.3 Marketing and Software Architectures: Layers, Partitions, and Platforms

management hierarchy as layers, and departments and teams that operate independently of each other as partitions—or, less flatteringly, silos. Like software, as organizations grow, they almost always embody a combination of these two structures.

But a particular kind of layer is special: a *platform*.

Platforms provide a common set of services and support capabilities to things built on the layer above. But they're more than that. Platforms define the boundaries of what can be built on top of them with a greater sense of shared purpose and functional coordination—yet empower individual creations at the layer above to flourish independently of each other.

Platforms excel at balancing cohesion and diversity.

From the previous chapter, we could view that as a balance of scalability and innovation. The platform is the *standard* that is exploited, while the things built on top of it can explore a diverse range of experimental possibilities—but within the platform's well-defined borders.

Apple's iPhone and iPad products are perfect examples of platforms in the software sense of the word. Through Apple's iOS operating system, which ensures that every app on one of its phones or tablets offers the same kind of user interface and plays nicely within that environment, it offers customers a beautifully cohesive mobile device. At the same time, Apple crafted an open technical foundation on which independent software developers could create apps that can seamlessly plug into their devices. And it established a distribution channel for selling those apps, the App Store, which has more than 1 million apps available—a spectacularly diverse set of choices for customers. This blend of cohesion and diversity has been key to Apple's success.

Platforms have also been used in manufacturing, such as in the automobile industry. A car platform—a common floor plan, wheelbase, steering mechanism, and powertrain—may serve as the foundation for a variety of models and marques.[7] For instance, the Toyota Camry and the Lexus ES sedans were built on the same platform.[8] This achieves economies of scale with shared components and greater returns from engineering investments in their mutual subsystems, while enabling creative differentiation for the vehicles built on those platforms.

Sangeet Paul Choudary, author of the book *Platform Scale*, suggests that, in the digital world, there are blossoming opportunities for more platform-like business models that serve as coordinated exchanges between producers and consumers primarily through managing and routing data and providing *a layer of shared supporting services* to both sides of the market.[9] He points to Airbnb, YouTube, Twitter, and Lyft—a competitor of Uber—as examples of this new kind of platform business. They bring value through a "network" layer rather than producing "stuff" themselves.[10]

Put another way, these platform businesses deliver consumers a reliable level of cohesion in their overall experience. But the actual goods and services exchanged are fulfilled by a diverse and largely independent set of producers. Facets of that diversity are often presented to consumers as a feature, giving them a wide range of choices to suit their individual preferences.

Again, great platforms brilliantly balance cohesion and diversity.

Platform Thinking in Marketing

Marketing has some experience with platforms too. Messaging platforms that define a brand's vision, positioning, and key points to communicate to the market have been used for many years to guide a variety of marketing communications. Marketing software platforms have been adopted for things such as website content management and marketing automation campaigns. And marketing certainly leverages social media platforms, such as Facebook, LinkedIn, Twitter, and YouTube, to engage with its audience.

But there are even greater opportunities for marketing to apply platform thinking to its internal capabilities and operations. Depending on the need for cohesion and diversity in a particular situation, and how they're balanced, as shown in Figure 23.4, platforms can play a powerful role in marketing management.

Traditionally, marketing has achieved much of its scale through partitions: different marketers working on different channels or programs, with relatively little coordination between them. We increasingly call those partitions silos, though, in an uncomplimentary fashion, because in today's interconnected digital world, partitions are often problematic. As customers glide among many channels and programs in a short window of time now, they expect a cohesive experience across all of them. From the outside, they view inconsistencies resulting from internal partitions as indifference or incompetence.

Of course, some partitioning is necessary as organizations grow larger. One way we can mitigate the downsides is by choosing our partitions with digital dynamics in mind. For instance, geographic regions are usually safer to partition than channels. Audience segments or stages of the buyer's journey may also provide more logical partition boundaries.

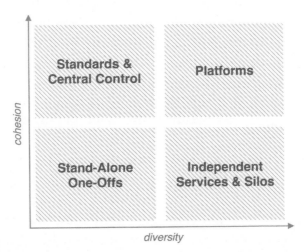

FIGURE 23.4   Platform-Thinking and the Relationship between Cohesion and Diversity

But in a world where everything is connected, no partition is an island.

An alternative is to consider how we can scale more through layers and, in particular, platforms. From a marketing management perspective, we can distinguish between the two this way. Layers, by themselves, provide hierarchy and governance. They establish boundaries and standards to help achieve cohesion in what's built on top of them.

Platforms, however, go further with three additional goals:

1. Augment the layer with more shared services, systems, and assets that the next layer up can use to build things—marketing campaigns, communications, and experiences—better and faster. Reusability and flexible modularity are typically two key aspects of platforms.
2. Provide the essential but lightweight coordination of the things built on top of them so that those things don't have to coordinate with each other individually—which would be hopelessly complex at scale. Platforms enable things at the next layer up to grow and evolve independently.
3. Encourage diversity so that the things built on top can vary widely from one another, within the constraints the platform establishes, but still with significant creative license.

By supporting those goals, platforms enable the creations built on top of them to adapt and evolve rapidly. Over time, the platform itself will likely evolve and adapt too—but usually on a slower timescale.

This leads us to the realization that pace layers in marketing are often natural boundaries around which platforms can be formed. For instance, thinking about a campaign as a *platform* changes what is provided to channels and tactics to enact it. Rather than prefab components and rigid blueprints for assembly, it's more like scaffolding, building blocks, a few starter kits or recommended design patterns, and access to on-demand construction services.

Instead of a precisely notated score for a symphony orchestra, think of chord charts that a jazz band would improvise around.

As a specific example, consider your company's e-mail marketing capabilities. If a single e-mail team directly executes all e-mail campaigns, that's a partition, a silo. However, if e-mail delivery is organized as more of a service that any marketer can take advantage of, using flexible templates, image libraries, a range of preapproved offer parameters, a service to define a recipient list from a centralized database, a scheduling calendar, a service to prevent different marketers in the company from repeatedly e-mailing the same recipients, an A/B testing feature to try alternative versions, standardized tracking and performance metrics, and so on, that's a platform.

An explosion of new marketing technologies is making it easier to create and support such marketing platforms on a technical level. But organizational structures, processes, and policies are still needed to implement these capabilities in a meaningful fashion.

More than anything, platform thinking is a shift in mind-set.

24

Taming Essential and Accidental Complexity in Marketing

F red Brooks is a famous software pioneer, renowned for his early insights about software development management. His book *The Mythical Man-Month* is a classic in the field that is still relevant today, more than 40 years later. It includes a maxim now known as Brooks' Law: "Adding manpower to a late software project makes it later."[1]

You may have experienced Brooks' Law yourself, even in a marketing context, when good-intentioned colleagues rush in to help with a project near the end—and it winds up costing you more time coordinating and communicating with that extra so-called help than the benefit received.

Brooks also wrote a widely celebrated essay, "No Silver Bullet—Essence and Accident in Software Engineering," that claimed there could be no single silver-bullet solution that by itself would achieve a 10× gain in software development productivity, reliability, or simplicity.[2]

The reason is that there are two kinds of complexity in software: *accidental complexity* and *essential complexity*.

Accidental complexity is the result of inevitable flaws in engineering, from minor bugs to subpar designs or architectures.

The example of the butterfly effect that we saw in the last chapter is an illustration of how accidental complexity can spiral out of hand, not just directly with software but with our processes that revolve around that software too.

Although there has been no silver bullet to solve accidental complexity, a combination of multiple management and technology improvements, such as agile and lean practices, have worked together to reduce accidental complexity over time. Reduce, but not eliminate, though, because the other kind of complexity keeps raising the bar.

As it turns out, the real digital dragon in software—and now marketing—is essential complexity.

Essential complexity is the complexity inherent in what we're trying to accomplish. As software has made it possible for us to tackle harder and more complicated problems, we have pursued ever greater software challenges. We started out using computers for basic bookkeeping, but now we apply elaborate machine learning algorithms to do predictive analytics on advanced financial models in real time.

The software ideas we pursue today are fundamentally more complex.

Marketing has experienced a similar explosion of essential complexity as well, largely because of entanglement in software-driven digital dynamics. An explosion of touchpoints, fragmentation of channels, acceleration in markets, expectations of more sophisticated customer experiences, the demand for data-driven accountability and optimization, and so on have made our profession intrinsically more complex. And as we conquer these challenges, we discover new mountains to climb on the horizon beyond.

Our reach always exceeds our grasp because we're always reaching further.

That's an admirable trait of the human spirit and an inescapable reality of competition. But it steadily expands the essential complexity that we have to manage.

Tame Essential Complexity with Purpose

There is really only one way to tame essential complexity in marketing: *simplify*.

I know, that sounds like Captain Obvious. But simplifying is actually extremely hard to do, especially when all the surrounding forces are pushing us toward greater complexity. It requires strength to push back yet wisdom to do so strategically. We don't want to impede progress, but we must focus our energy carefully.

With that in mind, we'll discuss three strategies for simplifying essential complexity.

First, choose what you do purposefully.

Arguably the single greatest management challenge of the twenty-first century is the divergence of the two curves in the graph illustrated here in Figure 24.1. The curve on top, which swings sharply upwards, is the rate at which technology is advancing, which is generally exponential for many digital technologies. This phenomenon is often attributed to Moore's Law: the approximate doubling of computing power every couple of years over the past 50 years.[3]

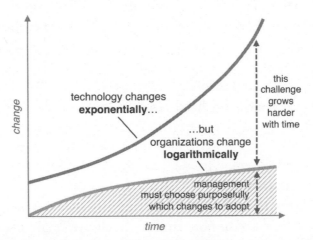

FIGURE 24.1 Martec's Law: Technology Changes Exponentially, but Organizations Change Logarithmically

The curve on bottom, however, rises at a much slower rate. It represents the notion that people and organizations generally do not change exponentially. Change is harder and slower for us humans. I draw this curve as a logarithm—it slows down as time goes on—because inertia seems to drag more heavily on an organization the longer it's been around.

Our challenge with these two curves growing apart is that there is more technological change happening in the world than any one organization can absorb. I dubbed this conundrum *Martec's Law*, because the pattern emerged as I observed marketing technologists wrestling with that dichotomy at companies trying to adopt increasingly sophisticated marketing software. But I believe it applies broadly to firms' struggles with accelerating technological innovation.

Given the fact that we cannot absorb all of these changes—at least not in the time frame in which they first appear—the only rational answer is to choose purposefully which ones we will embrace, and which ones we won't, at a given time. If we don't consciously make those judgments, what ends up under the curve in our organization becomes subject to chance.

Making these choices is easier said than done, however. We need a clear strategy, in the sense of AG Lafley and Roger Martin's adage that "Strategy is choice."[4] A good strategy establishes a framework by which we can decide what we will do and what we won't. We must then ruthlessly apply those criteria to select only a subset of innovations that are the best fit.

Those can still be hard choices, even if the logic behind them is clear. It's always tempting to try to embrace more. We must emphasize that it's okay—and even necessary—to leave other innovations unaddressed, to focus on the ones that matter most to our business.

Revisiting the concept of the edge and the core from Chapter 22, it's important to note that these choices primarily apply to what we bring into our core as a part of our foundational capabilities. It's the core that we're most concerned about simplifying.

It's actually good for marketing's activities on the edge to explore above the curve. Learning from those experiments helps inform our decisions about which innovations will be most effective for us to adopt more broadly. They also provide important, early signals that can influence the evolution of our strategy and the framework by which we make these choices. But as long as they're on the edge, we limit the attention and resources allocated to them.

One more factor that can help in considering which innovations to adopt, and when, is the diffusion of innovations curve by Everett Rogers.[5] This view of how innovations spread divides adopters into five categories, according to how quickly they embrace a new innovation: innovators, early adopters, early majority, late majority, and laggards. It's a well-known model in the technology industry, mostly from the point of view of companies trying to sell new products. It's also where Geoffrey Moore identified the challenge of "crossing the chasm"—the difficulty in bridging from purchases by early adopters to widespread adoption by the early majority.[6] This is illustrated in Figure 24.2.

From the point of view of being an adopter, though, we can choose where along that adoption curve we want to embrace a particular innovation. Generally speaking, we will wrestle with

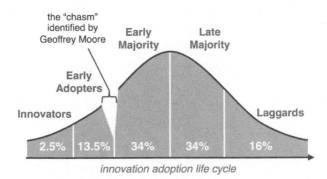

innovation adoption life cycle

An organization doesn't have to operate in a single category —it can be an **early adopter** in regard to some innovations and in the **late majority** for others. This may vary by team.

FIGURE 24.2 Everett Rogers's Model for the Diffusion of Innovations

more complexity as an early adopter than we will as a late majority adopter, because over time, products are improved, best practices are established, and the early kinks get worked out.

A crucial point, however, is that we don't have to fit into one category for everything we do. Strategically, we can choose to be an early adopter for some innovations and a laggard for others, depending on their relevance and relative priority to our business.

Resist Overengineering; Embrace Sunsetting

The next two strategies for simplifying essential complexity come into play after we have decided to adopt an innovation into marketing's core.

First, *don't overengineer.*

Overengineering is when something is built with more features, or for a significantly larger scale or scope, than what is actually known to be needed in the present day. Although it is often well intentioned as a way to prepare for the future, the downside is that it tends to cause far greater complexity. And because predicting the future is hard—especially in fast-changing environments, such as marketing and software—the scenarios for which we build that additional complexity often don't happen or at least not the way we originally imagined they might.

We pay the cost for unnecessary complexity without reaping the benefits.

This has been a constant struggle in software, which is why agile software development methodologies strive to prevent overengineering through principles such as building incrementally. The agile methodology known as *extreme programming* popularized the saying "You aren't gonna need it"—often referred to by its acronym, YAGNI—among programmers to remind each other that most complexity added in anticipation of something not yet here is waste.[7]

The engineering design principle KISS—"Keep it simple, stupid"—has advocated this same philosophy for decades and for good reason.[8] Build only what you need.

Marketing increasingly must battle overengineering now too.

This directly applies to the design and deployment of software and systems within marketing. But overengineering can also arise in organizational structures, processes, and policies. One of the reasons to leave projects and programs on the edge for an extended period is to avoid the complexity of building them up as core capabilities before we're certain that the investment is worth it. And when things do move into the core, we want to apply some restraint in how quickly we increase their scale or advance their maturity.

As an example of applying this strategy: Don't create excessively complex marketing automation campaigns unless it's demonstrably beneficial to do so. Gratuitous personalization logic, overly narrow audience segmentation, and a multitude of trigger events can all too easily complicate the operation and maintenance of campaigns without delivering a commensurate lift to your results.

Now, this doesn't mean we should *underengineer* marketing either. But we must balance the goal of scaling core marketing with the goal of keeping essential complexity down to only what we truly need.

The second strategy for simplifying essential complexity is *sunsetting*.

Sunsetting is the term used in software for shutting down old systems and deprecating old features. The basic idea is that if we aren't really using something, either because we replaced it with something else or because it's no longer relevant or important to our business, we can simplify our operations by eliminating it. It becomes one less thing to administer, support, and maintain.

In marketing, this applies not only to software but also to things such as content, Web pages, marketing automation programs, programmatic ad campaigns, reports, databases, social media outposts, and so on. Every external touchpoint or internal service that marketing is responsible for contributes to the overall complexity of its operations. Sunsetting things that we no longer need is a rational way to simplify.

However, this too is easier said than done.

It takes effort to sunset things. First we have to review what's in place and decide what should be sunsetted. Then there's the work of actually removing it or turning it off. That may involve archiving old assets or data, updating things that were connected to or dependent on it, notifying people affected by the change, and migrating any remaining use cases that still must be supported to something else. Aside from the logistics involved, there can also be people issues to address, from change management to the politics of people's pet projects.

But if we don't sunset things aggressively enough, we either get bogged down by legacy maintenance tasks or, if we just ignore them, increase the risk that things drifting unmaintained will accidentally cause bad experiences for customers—and we may not even realize it.

If you have out-of-date content on your website, this is a real problem you already have.

We have a finite amount of energy that we can apply to our marketing operations. If we keep adding new innovations in on one side, we need to transition out older things on the other side, ideally in an orderly fashion. This primarily applies to things in marketing's core. But junk can accumulate even more easily in the edge, so regular cleanups of discontinued experiments are a good idea.

Collectively, these three strategies—(1) *choose purposefully* which innovations to adopt, and avoid taking on too many at once; (2) *don't overengineer* the innovations that you do adopt; and (3) *intentionally sunset* the outdated elements of your portfolio—are the principal ways to simplify marketing's essential complexity.

Put more simply: do fewer things, and do them well.

Five Ways to Tame Accidental Complexity

Essential complexity is the hardest to manage, but accidental complexity is still tricky.

There's no silver bullet, but we can apply many techniques to keep accidental complexity in check. Here are five practices from the software community that lend themselves well to marketing's complexity too.

First, *refactoring*. Refactoring software is the practice of re-writing it—not to change what it does, but to improve its internal organization to make it easier to extend and maintain.[9] In a marketing context, the first way that we implement a program or campaign, particularly one that is configured through software, is often not the best approach. While figuring out how to do something at first, we can inadvertently construct it in a way that's unnecessarily complex. However, as we learn and gain more experience, we often benefit from going back and refactoring it. This is especially valuable for marketing elements that are going to be reused or serve as a template for others. A little investment in refactoring today can save a lot of time trouble-shooting tomorrow.

Second, *pair marketing*. In software, this is actually *pair programming*. Two developers work together to write a piece of code, with one as the "driver" at the keyboard and the other as the "observer."[10] We can apply the same idea for building marketing programs and campaigns, especially those that are programmatic in nature. The benefits of doing this are threefold: (1) The observer provides perspective that often results in a better implementation, (2) explaining your approach to another person usually helps you understand your own thinking more clearly, and (3) this practice helps spread knowledge and cross-pollinate ideas across different people on the team. If these joint walk-throughs are done after the fact in software, they're called code reviews. In marketing, we might call them *program reviews*.

If you don't have a partner, but you're trying to think through a complex implementation, you can get some of the benefit by explaining it out loud to an imaginary observer. In software circles, this is known as *rubber duck debugging*—actually explaining it to a rubber duck.[11]

Yes, it's a little funny. But it works.

Third, *loosely coupled designs.* As we discussed in the previous chapter, there are often many connections among different components in marketing. But this gets problematic when one thing changes and triggers a wave of ripple effects. Although we can't eliminate this complexity completely, because things do have to interconnect, we can reduce it by consciously trying to minimize the dependencies between components. For the dependencies that we do need, we strive to make them explicit rather than implicit, turning hidden assumptions into visible and well-defined handoffs. More broadly, we design for change. When we implement a new component in marketing, we consider the possibility that it, or any of the things it depends on, may need to be replaced at some point. We try to avoid doing things that would unnecessarily complicate such substitutions.

Fourth, *exception management* or *bulletproofing.* Novice software developers commonly make the mistake of thinking through what happens only in the normal case of their programs, without contemplating the ways in which things can go wrong. More experienced developers, on the other hand, implement their code defensively, so their programs can gracefully recover when something unexpected occurs. We can make our marketing programs and operations more resilient by considering possible exceptions in our designs and implementations too—taking reasonable steps to protect against them and still preserve the quality of customer experiences as much as possible.

And fifth, *built-in testing and monitoring.* When preparing new or updated releases in our marketing programs or campaigns, it's wise to have a way to test that they will work as expected. Simply trying it once yourself is better than nothing, but that's often insufficient. A more robust approach is to map out a variety of test scenarios—for instance, how does a landing page look on a smartphone as well as a larger computer screen?—and systematically verify them all. In software development, this is often known as *unit testing*.[12] Some marketing software can help you automate or semiautomate such tests, for greater efficiency and consistency. Additionally, it is often highly valuable to set up automated monitoring of ongoing programs and touchpoints so that if something suddenly stops working, you're quickly alerted. "Set it and forget it" marketing programs are usually better treated as "Trust but verify."

There are certainly many more techniques to fight accidental complexity in marketing and software, but if you can incorporate those five, you'll be off to a great start. I'd encourage you to continually exchange new ideas with your peers, as well as talk with software developers regularly to learn what new techniques they're seeing work in their profession.

Complexity is arguably the single greatest operational challenge of modern marketing. If you can master it, that's an incredible competitive advantage.

V

Talent

25

Chasing the Myth of the 10× Marketer

There's a persistent "myth" in software development: Great developers are 10× more productive than average developers.

I call it a "myth" in quotation marks because there's disagreement around that statement in the software community. For one thing, it's hard to measure the difference precisely. Is it 2×, 3×, or 5× instead? And second, the adoption of agile management has tended to emphasize the productivity of teams and to downplay the notion of the solo rock star programmer.

However, precision and popularity aside, it's basically true.

The best software developers *do* have an outsized impact on their organizations.

It's interesting to note that this myth actually got started by Fred Brooks, mentioned in the previous chapter, in his essay "No Silver Bullet." Although Brooks didn't believe that any one management technique or technology innovation could have a tenfold impact on software, he did believe that great talent could achieve that kind of effect: "The differences are not minor—it is rather like Salieri and Mozart. Study after study shows that the very best designers produce structures that are faster, smaller, simpler, cleaner, and produced with less effort.

The difference between the great and the average approach an order of magnitude."[1]

Brooks reasoned that organizations would be best served by focusing on finding and nurturing that talent. Indeed, most of the world's best software companies today do just that, as observed in the heated recruiting battles between firms such as Apple, Facebook, and Google.

But to connect this with marketing, there are actually two factors to this outsized impact. The first is talent, but the second is the *leverage* that digital dynamics, especially speed and scale, provide to that talent. Great software can spread 10× further. It can solve problems in the digital space 10× faster or with 10× greater accuracy. The nature of the digital canvas is what enables those talented developers to shine.

Marketing has always had plenty of amazing talent too.

What has changed, however, is that digital dynamics in marketing now give more talent in marketing access to this tremendous new leverage. Brilliant content and campaigns can go viral and achieve outsized returns, even with limited budgets and resources. The smart use of marketing automation can multiply the number of customer touchpoints that a single marketer can effectively orchestrate by an order of magnitude. The number of marketing experiments that can be run in a given year—to explore more opportunities for innovation, more rapidly, and more efficiently—can increase many times over.

The digital world, and the convergence that's brought between marketing and software, has now enabled the rise of the *10× marketer.*

Like in software, that will surely be a "myth" to some degree too, of course. Marketing is best executed as a team sport, and for many marketing metrics, 10× would be an unreasonable goal. But it's a myth worth chasing, because even a fraction of such accelerated growth—2× or 3×—by individuals and small teams will have spectacular impact on a business's success.

Empowering Modern Marketers

What Fred Brooks stated for software developers, we can now restate for marketers: In a digital world, *people* are the most important factor to marketing's success. Finding, developing, and nurturing great talent is the ultimate source of competitive advantage in modern marketing.

This has always been true, of course. But because of the leverage of digital dynamics, it's now 10× truer. Brains trump budgets in a digital world.

The fierce competition for marketers will increasingly mirror the race we've seen for great software developers. It won't be only marketing executives who are highly sought after but marketers at all levels who are able to wield digital dynamics successfully as a force multiplier.

To attract, develop, and retain that talent—and, really, to harness the potential that they have to offer—organizations must focus on empowering these digital-world marketers as the key to competitive advantage. Most of the practices we've covered in this book for achieving high-performance marketing agility and innovation revolve around that principle.

Agile marketing, at its heart, is about giving individual marketers and small marketing teams greater ownership of their work and significant latitude in how they achieve their goals. It operates on trust and transparency, more than command and control. It gives marketers at all levels visibility into how their pieces fit into the strategy of the whole. And it gives them the opportunity to contribute to its evolution.

The innovation techniques of collaborative design and big testing that we covered earlier are about democratizing the exploration of new ideas. Every marketer is encouraged to experiment, iterate, and learn. By structuring scalability into the edge and the core, we facilitate innovation on a broader basis, without sacrificing the reliability or efficiency of our foundational capabilities.

Everybody innovates. Everybody learns. Everybody grows.

This is the kind of work environment that has thrilled software developers—the chance to work on exciting and meaningful projects, see how they're having an impact, and take pride in making a difference. They get to push themselves and their organizations to new levels. They get to learn, explore, and collaborate. They get to create, invent, and discover.

The world's best software companies, both large and small, from start-ups to Internet giants, compete mightily to offer developers the most attractive environments of this kind.

Companies craving the best marketing talent will increasingly do the same.

It's not primarily a competition over salaries, bonuses, stock options, or perks. Those are factors, but they're often the least differentiated elements in the talent market. It's much more a competition of passion and imagination. The companies that are best able to stir the minds and souls of the marketers they seek—and give them powerful organizational platforms on which to achieve great things—will dominate the talent war of modern marketing.

The Full-Stack Marketer

The last concept from the software community that we'll borrow and adapt in this book is the idea of a full-stack developer and the parallel of a *full-stack marketer*.

A full-stack developer is capable of working in all the different functional layers that make up a modern software program: not only the application logic but also the underlying database, the user interface, quality assurance testing, and even the processes for deploying the software into production systems.

Of course, in many cases, a full-stack developer will have greater expertise in one or two of those layers. But they understand how all the layers fit together, and they can contribute to any of them as needed. If necessary, with a project of reasonable size, they could build the entire program themselves. That's powerful flexibility.

These are T-shaped people: deep in at least one area but proficient across many.

There is a wide range of new specializations in marketing these days, brought about by the explosion of channels and technologies in our profession. There are marketers who specialize in areas such as social media and content marketing. There are marketers who specialize in technical disciplines, such as marketing technologists, creative technologists, data scientists, and growth hackers.

As new disruptive innovations continue to arise in marketing, even more new specialties will emerge. Some will be new titles. Some will be new skills. And some will simply be new ways of thinking.

There is genuine depth within these specialties, and the people who acquire expertise in them are highly valuable—especially if they're slightly ahead of the curve, as those capabilities become increasingly demanded by many, but few professionals have mastered them yet.

At the same time, however, the bar is continually raised for what we expect of baseline generalist marketers, as shown in Figure 25.1. "Digital marketer" was once a specialization, and marketers without that title were not expected to be fluent in digital skills. But today, *every* marketer is expected to be proficient in basic digital marketing knowledge.

Many of the specialties of the present day are also steadily migrating key concepts and skills back into baseline marketing competencies. Today's generalist marketers are increasingly required to be social media savvy, technology savvy, and data savvy.

For a number of these specialties, marketers may never be expected to be experts. But they are expected to understand where those specialties fit in the overall architecture of modern

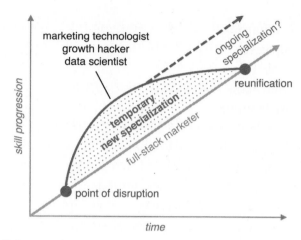

FIGURE 25.1   Marketing Specializations and the Baseline of a Full-Stack Marketer

marketing. They are increasingly expected to be able to perform some of the basic tasks of those specialties as needed and to contribute flexibly across the full stack of modern marketing.

They are full-stack marketers.

These full-stack marketers are immensely valuable. But they don't come prepackaged from business schools. They're developed through the hands-on practice of agile marketing and democratized innovation. The opportunity to experiment, learn, and grow across a wide spectrum of marketing projects and programs is what produces great full-stack marketers.

Hacking Marketing

This is a fascinating time to work in marketing.

Although the tremendous pace of change around us can sometimes be uncomfortable, there has never been a greater time in marketing history for individual marketers to personally effect change—in their companies, in their careers, and in the profession as a whole.

Digital dynamics have given us digital leverage and the rise of the 10× marketer.

This book is titled *Hacking Marketing* for three reasons. First, the remarkable confluence of software and marketing has opened up an inspiring source of ideas that we can cross-pollinate between these two great professions. Second, the creative spirit of hacking—the good kind of hacking—champions a willingness to defy old conventions and reimagine what's possible. And third, hacking favors a strong bias for action. We may not have all the answers to the challenges we face, but if we're undaunted and willing to experiment and learn, we can discover new and innovative ways forward.

You've reached the end of this book, but hopefully it's just the beginning of your journey into the future of marketing.

The horizon awaits you.

And remember, hacking is a good thing.

Notes

Chapter 1

1. Facebook, "Form S-1 Registration Statement: Facebook, Inc.," February 1, 2012. www.sec.gov/Archives/edgar/data/1326801/000119312512034517/d287954ds1.htm.
2. Brian Harvey, "What Is a Hacker?" Accessed November 23, 2015, www.cs.berkeley.edu/~bh/hacker.html.

Chapter 2

1. Jack Neff, "K-C: 'We Don't Believe in Digital Marketing. . . [But] Marketing in a Digital World.'" *Advertising Age*, March 21, 2012. http://adage.com/article/cmo-strategy/kimberly-clark-elevates-clive-sirkin-top-marketing-post/233451/.
2. Jamie Truscott-Howell, "Carat Predicts Digital Spend to Reach More Than 25% of Total Advertising Spend in 2016," Carat, March 24, 2015. www.carat.com/uk/en/news-views/carat-predicts-digital-spend-to-reach-more-than-25-of-total-advertising-spend-in-2016/.
3. Shar VanBoskirk, "US Digital Marketing Will Pass TV in Two Years, Topping $100B by 2019," Forrester Research, November 6, 2014. http://blogs.forrester.com/shar_vanboskirk/14–11–06-us_digital_marketing_will_pass_tv_in_two_years_topping_100b_by_2019.
4. Graham Charlton, 2015. "77% of Businesses Plan to Increase Digital Marketing Budgets This Year," Econsultancy, February 26, 2015. https://econsultancy.com/blog/66135–77-of-businesses-plan-to-increase-digital-marketing-budgets-this-year/.

Chapter 3

1. There are some technical exceptions to this. Digital precision holds true only when dealing with discrete numbers—integers—up to a certain

size. When working with real numbers, numbers with decimal places, we run into issues with rounding errors. With large numbers, we can encounter arithmetic overflow problems, where a number gets arbitrarily cut off or wraps around into a smaller number. Finally, when we digitally measure physical world phenomena, we face challenges with the accuracy and precision of our measurements as they're being captured.

Chapter 4

1. Maurizio Pesce, "Software Takes on More Tasks in Today's Cars," *WIRED*, April 25, 2011. www.wired.com/2011/04/the-growing-role-of-software-in-our-cars.

2. Adrian Colyer, "Grady Booch's Keynote at AOSD," *The Aspect Blog*, March 16, 2005. www.aspectprogrammer.org/blogs/adrian/2005/03/grady_boochs_ke.html.

3. Chuck Rossi, "Ship Early and Ship Twice as Often," Facebook, August 3, 2012. https://www.facebook.com/notes/facebook-engineering/ship-early-and-ship-twice-as-often/10150985860363920.

4. O'Reilly, "Velocity 2011: Jon Jenkins, 'Velocity Culture,'" YouTube video, 15:13, June 20, 2011. www.youtube.com/watch?v=dxk8b9rSKOo.

Chapter 5

1. Ingrid Lunden, "IFTTT Launches 3 'Do' Apps to Automate Photo Sharing, Tasks, Notes; Rebrands Main App 'IF,'" TechCrunch, February 19, 2015. http://techcrunch.com/2015/02/19/ifttt-launches-3-do-apps-to-automate-photo-sharing-tasks-notes-rebrands-main-app-if.

Chapter 8

1. *Oxford English Dictionary*, s.v. "Agile." Accessed August 6, 2015. www.oxforddictionaries.com/us/definition/english/agile.

2. Kent Beck, Mike Beedle, Arie van Bennekum, Alistair Cockburn, Ward Cunningham, Martin Fowler, and James Grenning et al, "Manifesto for Agile Software Development," February, 2001. www.agilemanifesto.org.

3. Jeff Sutherland, Dilip Patel, Cory Casanave, Glenn Hollowell, and Joaquin Miller, eds., *Business Object Design and Implementation: OOPSLA '95 Workshop Proceedings* (New York: Springer, 1997), 118.

4. Taiichi Ohno, *Toyota Production System: Beyond Large-Scale Production* (Cambridge, MA: Productivity Press, 1988).

5. David J. Anderson, *Agile Management for Software Engineering: Applying the Theory of Constraints for Business Results* (Upper Saddle River, NJ: Prentice Hall, 2004).

6. Corey Ladas, "Scrum-Ban," Lean Software Engineering, July 2008. http://leansoftwareengineering.com/ksse/scrum-ban/.

7. Eric Ries, *The Lean Startup: How Today's Entrepreneurs Use Continuous Innovation to Create Radically Successful Businesses* (New York: Crown Business, 2011).

8. Matt Blumberg, "Agile Marketing," *Only Once* (blog), February 28, 2006. www.onlyonceblog.com/2006/02/agile_marketing.

9. Scott Brinker, "Ideas for an Agile Marketing Manifesto," *Chief Marketing Technologist Blog*, March 24, 2010. http://chiefmartec.com/2010/03/ideas-for-an-agile-marketing-manifesto.

10. The "Agile Marketing Manifesto" is available at http://agilemarketing manifesto.org.

Chapter 11

1. Oreo, Twitter post, February 3, 2013, 5:48 PM. https://twitter.com/oreo/status/298246571718483968.

Chapter 12

1. Scott Brinker, "Agile Marketing for Conversion Optimization," Search Engine Land, March 24, 2010. http://searchengineland.com/agile-marketing-for-conversion-optimization-37902.

2. Facebook, "Form S-1 Registration Statement: Facebook, Inc," February 1, 2012. www.sec.gov/Archives/edgar/data/1326801/000119312512034517/d287954ds1.htm.

Chapter 13

1. Karen Martin, and Mike Osterling, *Value Stream Mapping: How to Visualize Work and Align Leadership for Organizational Transformation* (New York: McGraw-Hill, 2014).

Chapter 14

1. Clayton M. Christensen, Scott Cook, and Taddy Hall, "Marketing Malpractice: The Cause and the Cure," *Harvard Business Review*, December 2005. https://hbr.org/2005/12/marketing-malpractice-the-cause-and-the-cure.
2. Carmen Nobel, "Clay Christensen's Milkshake Marketing," *HBS Working Knowledge*, February 14, 2001. http://hbswk.hbs.edu/item/6496.html.
3. The Fibonacci sequence is 1, 1, 2, 3, 5, 8, 13, 21, and so on. Each subsequent number is the sum of the previous two numbers before it, such as 8 + 13 = 21.

Chapter 15

1. Alan Deutschman, "Inside the Mind of Jeff Bezos," Fast Company, August 2004. www.fastcompany.com/50106/inside-mind-jeff-bezos.
2. Robert K. Greenleaf, *Servant Leadership: A Journey into the Nature of Legitimate Power & Greatness*, 25th anniversary ed. (New York: Paulist Press, 2002).

Chapter 16

1. Don Wells, "The Rules of Extreme Programming," 1999. www.extremeprogramming.org/rules.html.
2. Alistair Cockburn and Laurie William, "The Costs and Benefits of Pair Programming," Proceedings of the First International Conference on Extreme Programming and Flexible Processes in Software Engineering (XP2000), 2000.
3. AG Lafley and Roger L. Martin, *Playing to Win: How Strategy Really Works* (Boston: Harvard Business Review Press, 2013).

Chapter 17

1. Some of my favorite agile and lean management books are *Scrum: The Art of Doing Twice the Work in Half the Time* by Jeff Sutherland, *Essential Scrum* by Kenneth S. Rubin, *Learning Agile* by Andrew Stellman and Jennifer Greene, *Lean Software Development* by Mary and Tom Poppendieck, and *Lean UX* by Jeff Gothelf and Josh Seiden.

Chapter 18

1. Marshall McLuhan, *Understanding Media: The Extensions of Man* (New York: New American Library, 1964).
2. Content Marketing Institut, "What Is Content Marketing?" Accessed November 24, 2015, http://contentmarketinginstitute.com/what-is-content-marketing.
3. Demand Metric, "Enhancing the Buyer's Journey: Benchmarks for Content & the Buyer's Journey," June 2014. www.demandmetric.com/content/content-buyers-journey-benchmark-report.
4. Bob L. Lord and Ray Velez, *Converge: Transforming Business at the Intersection of Marketing and Technology* (Hoboken, NJ: John Wiley & Sons, 2013).

Chapter 19

1. Andrew Chen, "The Law of Shitty Clickthroughs." Accessed November 24, 2015, http://andrewchen.co/the-law-of-shitty-clickthroughs.
2. With my apologies to Eric Ries.

Chapter 20

1. Andrew Chen, "The Law of Shitty Clickthroughs." Accessed November 24, 2015, http://andrewchen.co/the-law-of-shitty-clickthroughs.
2. Clayton M. Christensen, Stephen P. Kaufman, and Willy C. Shih, "Innovation Killers: How Financial Tools Destroy Your Capacity to Do New Things," *Harvard Business Review*, January 2008.

https://hbr.org/2008/01/innovation-killers-how-financial-tools-destroy-your-capacity-to-do-new-things/ar/1.

3. Larry Page, and Sergey Brin, "Amendment No. 9 to Form S-1 Registration Statement: Google Inc.," August 18, 2004. www.sec.gov/Archives/edgar/data/1288776/000119312504142742/ds1a.htm.

4. Natalie Zmuda, "Why You Don't Need to Fear—and May Even Want to Embrace—the F Word: Failure," *AdvertisingAge*, October 8, 2012. http://adage.com/article/news/fear-f-word-failure/237618.

5. Slack, Twitter post, February 7, 2014, 10:48 a.m. https://twitter.com/SlackHQ/status/431862004895076352.

6. *Wikipedia*, s.v., "5 Whys." Last modified October 15, 2015; accessed November 8, 2015. https://en.wikipedia.org/wiki/5_Whys.

7. Steve Gary Blank, *The Four Steps to the Epiphany: Successful Strategies for Products That Win* (Foster City, CA: Cafepress.com, 2005).

8. Eric Von Hippel, "Lead Users: A Source of Novel Product Concepts," *Management Science* 32, no. 7 (1986): 791–806. doi:10.1287/mnsc.32.7.791.

9. Steven Johnson, *Where Good Ideas Come From: The Natural History of Innovation* (New York: Riverhead Books, 2010).

Chapter 21

1. Jeffrey P. Bezos, "Exhibit 99.1," April 2014. https://www.sec.gov/Archives/edgar/data/1018724/000119312514137753/d702518dex991.htm.

2. Jim Manzi, *Uncontrolled: The Surprising Payoff of Trial-and-Error for Business, Politics, and Society* (New York: Basic Books, 2012).

3. Avinash Kaushik, "Seven Steps to Creating a Data Driven Decision Making Culture," *Occam's Razor* (blog), October 23, 2006. www.kaushik.net/avinash/seven-steps-to-creating-a-data-driven-decision-making-culture.

Chapter 22

1. Gartner, "Bimodal IT," 2013. Accessed October 27, 2015. www.gartner.com/it-glossary/bimodal.

2. Capability Maturity Model and CMM are registered in the U.S. Patent and Trademark Office by Carnegie Mellon University.

3. *Wikipedia*, s.v., "Capability Maturity Model," Last modified November 24, 2015; accessed November 27, 2015. https://en.wikipedia.org/wiki/Capability_Maturity_Model.

Chapter 23

1. *Wikipedia*, s.v., "Butterfly Effect." Last modified October 27, 2015; accessed November 1, 2015. https://en.wikipedia.org/wiki/Butterfly_effect.
2. Stewart Brand, *How Buildings Learn: What Happens After They're Built* (New York: Viking Penguin, 2014).
3. Stewart Brand, *The Clock of the Long Now: Time and Responsibility* (New York: Basic Books, 1999).
4. Gartner, "Pace-Layered Application Strategy," 2013. Accessed November 2, 2015, www.gartner.com/it-glossary/pace-layered-application-strategy.
5. Jesse James Garrett, *The Elements of User Experience: User-Centered Design for the Web* (Indianapolis: New Riders, 2002).
6. Scott Brinker, "A 2-Sided Silver Bullet for Marketing and Sales Alignment?" *Chief Marketing Technologist Blog*, April 17, 2015. http://chiefmartec.com/2015/04/new-approach-challenge-salesmarketing-alignment.
7. Michael Brylawski, "Uncommon Knowledge: Automotive Platform Sharing's Potential Impact on Advanced Technologies," Abstract. Paper presented at the International Society for the Advancement of Material and Process Engineering Automotive Conference, Detroit, September 27–29, 1999. www.rmi.org/Knowledge-Center/Library/T99–10_UncommonKnowledge.
8. Phil Edmonston, *Lemon-Aid: Used Cars and Minivans 2004* (Toronto: Penguin Group, 2003).
9. Sangeet Paul Choudary, *Platform Scale: How an Emerging Business Model Helps Startups Build Large Empires with Minimum Investment* (Singapore: Platform Thinking Labs, 2015).
10. Sangeet Paul Choudary, "A Platform-Thinking Approach to Innovation," *WIRED*, January, 2014. www.wired.com/insights/2014/01/platform-thinking-approach-innovation.

Chapter 24

1. Frederick P. Brooks, Jr., *The Mythical Man-Month* (Reading, MA: Addison-Wesley, 1975).
2. Frederick P. Brooks, Jr., "No Silver Bullet—Essence and Accident in Software Engineering," in *Information Processing 86: Proceedings of the IFIP 10th World Computer Congress, Dublin, Ireland, September 1–5, 1986*, ed. Hans-Jürgen Kugler (Amsterdam, Netherlands: Elsevier Science, 1986), 1069–1076.

3. *Wikipedia*, s.v., "Moore's Law." Last modified November 28, 2015; accessed November 28, 2015. https://en.wikipedia.org/wiki/Moore%27s_law.

4. AG Lafley and Roger L. Martin, *Playing to Win: How Strategy Really Works* (Boston: Harvard Business Review Press, 2013).

5. Everett M. Rogers, *Diffusion of Innovations*, 5th ed (New York: Simon & Schuster, 2003).

6. Geoffrey A. Moore, *Crossing the Chasm: Marketing and Selling High-Tech Products to Mainstream Customers* (New York: HarperCollins, 1991).

7. Ron Jeffries, Ann Anderson, and Chet Hendrickson, *Extreme Programming Installed* (Boston, MA: Addison-Wesley Professional, 2000).

8. *Wikipedia*, s.v., "KISS Principle." Last modified November 24, 2015; accessed November 28, 2015. https://en.wikipedia.org/wiki/KISS_principle.

9. *Wikipedia*, s.v., "Code Refactoring." Last modified September 21, 2015; accessed November 8, 2015. https://en.wikipedia.org/wiki/Code_refactoring.

10. Laurie Williams, "Integrating Pair Programming into a Software Development Process," in *14th Conference on Software Engineering Education and Training: Proceedings*, ed. Dawn Ramsey, Pierre Bourque, and Robert Dupuis (Los Alamitos, CA: IEEE Computer Society, 2001), 27–36.

11. *Wikipedia*, s.v., "Rubber Duck Debugging." Last modified November 6, 2015; accessed November 8, 2015. https://en.wikipedia.org/wiki/Rubber_duck_debugging.

12. *Wikipedia*, s.v., "Unit Testing." Last modified November 17, 2015; accessed November 28, 2015. https://en.wikipedia.org/wiki/Unit_testing.

Chapter 25

1. Frederick P. Brooks, Jr., 1986. "No Silver Bullet—Essence and Accident in Software Engineering," in *Information Processing 86: Proceedings of the IFIP 10th World Computer Congress, Dublin, Ireland, September 1–5, 1986*, ed. Hans-Jürgen Kugler (Amsterdam, Netherlands: Elsevier Science, 1986), 1069–1076.

Acknowledgments

Writing this book has been a humbling experience.

In examining the fascinating confluence of marketing and technology—a passion I've nurtured for most of my career—I've drawn upon hundreds, more likely thousands, of sources of inspiration. In the process of attempting to synthesize those pieces into a coherent narrative, I have had the opportunity to reflect on a lifetime's worth of lessons that I've been fortunate to learn from so many teachers and fellow travelers along the way.

My gratitude for all of the people who have contributed to my mental models of modern marketing management is immense—yet, sadly, exceeds my ability to remember them all for the credit they deserve here. I hope those whom I neglect to mention by name will forgive me. But because done is better than perfect (hacking credits), I'll offer the following thank-yous with the caveat that they are woefully incomplete.

First and foremost, thank you to some of the giants whose shoulders I have stood upon: Steve Blank, Stewart Brand, Fred Brooks, Clay Christensen, Seth Godin, Ron Jeffries, Eric Ries, Ken Schwaber, Jeff Sutherland, Ohno Taiichi, Nassim Nicholas Taleb, and Mark Zuckerberg.

Thank you to the agile marketing community, especially Travis Arnold, Matt Blumberg, John Cass, Jason Cohen, Frank Days, Jim Ewel, Jeff Gothelf, Barre Hardy, Greg Meyer, Mike McKinnon, Neil Perkin, David Quinn, Roland Smart, Miguel Tam, Jascha Kaykas-Wolff, Mark Verone, and Mike Volpe.

Thank you to the many marketing and technology superstars who have influenced my thinking on these topics, including

Vala Afshar, Neeraj Agrawal, Marc Andreessen, David Armano, Jay Baer, Jonathan Becher, Andrew Chen, Jeff Cram, Jeff Eckman, David Edelman, Bryan Eisenberg, Ashley Friedlein, Ashu Garg, Frank Gilbane, Mayur Gupta, Ann Handley, Jason Heller, Jane Hiscock, Gord Hotchkiss, Brian Kardon, Michael Krigsman, Jim Lecinski, Lance Loveday, Laura McLellan, Sheldon Monteiro, Gerry Murray, Joe Pulizzi, David Raab, Paul Roetzer, Robert Rose, Erica Seidel, Dharmesh Shah, Patrick Spenner, Cory Treffiletti, Ray Velez, Jeremy Waite, Steve Woods, and Isaac Wyatt.

Thank you to my colleagues at ion interactive, especially Eric Amodio, Jason Palter, Anna Talerico, and Justin Talerico, with whom I've had many inspiring conversations over many years. It's been a joy bringing products to life with you, shaping a new generation of marketing.

Thank you to Chris Elwell, Danny Sullivan, and the team at Third Door Media who produce the MarTech conference series, which has brought together an amazing community of professionals at the intersection of marketing and technology from all around the world.

Thank you to my Massachusetts Institute of Technology Sloan Fellows forum for their support and encouragement.

Thank you to my editors at John Wiley & Sons, Shannon Vargo and Elizabeth Gildea, for taking a chance on what surely must have sounded like a bizarre project ("Hacking marketing?"), and to the entire team involved in the production of this book.

An enormous thank-you to Chris Robert, a lifelong friend and collaborator, who offered incredibly valuable feedback on the early versions of this book and has enthusiastically engaged in years of discussions with me on these topics. Thank you also to our late mentor, Tim Stryker.

Of course, thank you to my parents for having always encouraged me to pursue my own path and being the ultimate source of my blended interests in marketing, software, writing, and entrepreneurship.

Most of all, thank you to my wife and daughter, Jill and Jordan, who patiently put up with me being sequestered most evenings and weekends, for many months, to bring this book to life. You are a tremendous blessing in my life, and I love you.

About the Author

Scott Brinker has more than 20 years' experience at the intersection of marketing and software. He is the editor of the *Chief Marketing Technologist* blog, chiefmartec.com, and the program chair of the MarTech conference series. He is a frequent keynote speaker on marketing and technology topics worldwide and has written articles published by *AdvertisingAge*, *Adweek*, *Harvard Business Review*, InformationWeek, TechCrunch, and VentureBeat.

Scott is also the cofounder and chief technology officer of ion interactive, a marketing software company that provides a platform for interactive content that has been adopted by many of the world's leading brands. Previously, he ran a Web development agency and led a pioneering electronic bulletin board system (BBS) software company. He started his career designing multiplayer online games.

Scott earned degrees in computer science from Columbia University and Harvard University and an MBA from MIT as a Sloan Fellow.

Index

Note: Page references in *italics* refer to figures.